The Security Man's Tale

By Mick Lee

First Published in 2017 by Michael Lee

Written by Michael Lee

Editing by Anne Grange at Wild Rosemary Writing
Services

Text and Photographs Copyright © Mick Lee 2017

ISBN-13:
978-1978032057

ISBN-10:
1978032056

To Christine, without whom…

My wedding to Christine in 1969.

With Christine, my best friend.

Introduction and Acknowledgements

This is my reminiscence. I've written it for the benefit of my grandchildren and any others that come after them; also for anyone else who may be interested.

It is a selfish tome, but I want to acknowledge that there have been many people without whose positive influence, I would have been set on the wrong road. Unfortunately, I can't mention all of them.

This book is by me, about me. However, there is one person without whom there would be no grandchildren, no business, and probably nothing to write about: Christine, my wife, business partner, mentor, critic, lover, friend and everything else for approaching fifty years.

Chapter 1: A Difficult Beginning

Me as a toddler – what a cheeky smile!

I was born on the 17th January 1948, in a nursing home in the centre of Sheffield. I was one of the first kids to be born under the auspices of the NHS. Apparently mine was a difficult birth and my poor mother was in labour for several days. A fact she continues to remind me about, despite the passing of nearly seventy years!

My father Fred was, at the time, a steelworker. My mother Joan had been a nurse during and after the Second World War. She came from a family of miners.

My mother Joan, as a teenager.

In those days, mining families split into two types: those who worked hard, drank and gambled, and those who went to the chapel, looked after their families, and prospered. Joan's father, Tom White, was from the latter type, a respected member of the Wesleyan congregation. He had six children and due to his frugality and prudence, managed to purchase, in cash, a house for each of his children on their marriage.

Joan's marriage to my father, Fred, was not welcome in her family as he was rightly perceived as being from a family of criminals. However, whilst this perception of the Lee family was correct, they were wrong in attributing these predilections to Fred.

Fred Lee as a young boy.

Our first family home was in Handsworth, Sheffield. The house is still standing and is in good repair. It was ideally situated, opposite a school and backing onto a recreation ground.

I have no clear memories of my parents' house in Handsworth, other than that it was shared by a pack of bull terriers, as my dad bred them. These dogs were my earliest guardians, playmates and babysitters.

I have a deep and sincere love of this breed of dog, and feel a familiarity with them which has on at least one occasion not been reciprocated and I have ended up getting a sharp nip for being over-friendly!

We lived in this house until I was about four years old, when my mum and dad bought the local chip shop. My dad worked full-time as a forge man at Firth Browns on Saville Street. He had worked there right the way through the Second World War, steel-working being a reserved occupation in regards to the vital work he was doing, producing the steel that made the armaments.

Fred Lee's parents were the licensees of the Norfolk pub on Saville Street, opposite the forge, so he was conveniently situated for his breaks and for a pint or two after work.

My father came from a long line of licensees. His father, my granddad George, had been at the Norfolk since the end of the First World War and had run the pub through the darkest days of the Sheffield gangs; indeed Princess Street, where the notorious murder involving the Fowler brothers happened in the 1920s, is within a few strides of the pub's front door.

George was one of three licensee brothers. I am said to resemble my Great Uncle Josh, who was above six feet in height and weighed over twenty stones – it is said that at his funeral, the pall bearers were struggling with his coffin and his wife Elsie was heard to say:

'Oh, Josh you have been an awkward bugger all your life and you're still as bad dead!' Amongst the mourners was a man known as Little Herbert. Herbert had been born disabled but managed to travel very quickly by use of a foot-propelled scooter, all three Lee brothers having pubs within a short walk of each other. When trouble started, it was Herbert's job to scoot along to the other brothers so they could bring reinforcements.

I know that the Lee family lived on the borders of the law. It was said that during the Second World War, George Lee had a fine stock of whatever you wanted, stored neatly in the ample cellars that ran beneath the pub. The railway yards were nearby and were easy prey for determined thieves. It was said the Norfolk's cellars were where the stolen property was stored.

I barely remember Granddad George; he was a heavy drinker and smoker, and not always a nice guy.

He died skint, coughing and confused when I was about five years old.

It is clear that George Lee was a crook. I have never quite managed to find out what his status was: he was never prosecuted, and he kept a pub license for many years. It is clear, however, that he was a leading receiver of stolen goods. Also, off-course bookmaking was illegal in those days and he made money supplying bookies' runners to the steelworks and mines.

Property could be ordered and indeed delivered via Grandad. It appears that Amazon had nothing on George Lee! The Norfolk was raided by civil and military police in 1944 and as a result, a number of men were imprisoned, but George avoided it all and kept his license.

During the dark days of the 1930s Depression, when millions of men were out of work, the Sheffield Gangs held sway throughout the city. Gambling was their main source of income, in the pitch and toss rings at Skye Edge, and elsewhere. They also ran protection rackets on racecourses throughout the north of England, extorting bookmakers and regularly causing serious disturbances.

My grandfather and his brothers were not members of these gangs and stood no nonsense from them. A family story from those times details the day when two gang members entered the Norfolk and, seeing the tap room full of unemployed men sharing a drink and passing round a single fag, threw a packet of twenty cigarettes onto the floor and dared someone to pick it up. George went round the bar, flattened the thugs, and passed the fags around himself.

My great-grandmother Hannah Lee, landlady of the Cricketers' Arms at Bramall Lane and the Ye Olde Shakespeare Inn in Heeley.

The Lees were of gypsy ancestry and you had only to look at the Lee women to see that was true. They were all beautiful women, with long dark hair and eyes of the darkest brown, almost black. Fiery, they were tolerant only of their husbands and older male relatives, and as such, they had a lot to put up with.

At least two of the Lee women were also licensees in their own right: My great-grandmother Hannah Lee had the Cricketers Arms on Bramall lane near the Sheffield United football ground; the other ran the Norfolk on Dixon Lane, adjacent to the rag and tag market, which again was a notorious centre for the disposal of stolen goods.

The family had connections in London, including a number of them who were in the Upton Park Gypsies, a gang that was heavily involved in the black market during the war, and before and after World

War Two, were involved in protection rackets at greyhound and horse racing tracks. Violet Lee was the mother of the infamous Kray twins – I think she was my grandfather's second cousin.

Another licensee relative was Lord Billy Lee, who kept the Traveller's Rest pub on the Moor in the 1920s. Lord Billy was of a different class. He had been a "turn" in the Music Halls as a song and dance man, retiring into the Travellers and from there running an artists' management business as well. I've seen photographs of Lord Billy with a bar decorated with aspidistras and other tropical plants, and waiters with long white aprons and trays standing behind him. Billy looks dapper, immaculate and well-heeled. He provided accommodation for touring artists in the pub, and family folklore tells a tale that one night Jack Johnson, former heavyweight Champion of the

World and Georges Carpentier, the French former light heavyweight World Champion had appeared at the Empire Music Hall and were staying overnight.

They were having a nightcap with Billy when the skylight opened and two burglars shimmied down a rope into the bar. Seeing Johnson and Carpentier, the men froze.

'If you can get out the same way you got in, we'll let you go,' Billy said.

Apparently they shot back up the rope as fast as they had descended. I've no idea if it's true, but there we are. Johnson certainly appeared with Carpentier at Sheffield's Empire Theatre in the early 1920s and may well have stayed with Lord Billy Lee. For perspective from a modern point of view, put yourself in the position of the burglars being confronted by Lennox Lewis *and* Mike Tyson at the same time!

Apparently, Lord Billy was a good friend of Carpentier, (known as the "Orchid Man", as he always had an orchid in his buttonhole). Billy travelled by ship to New York to see him fight Jack Dempsey for the world title in the 20s, so it may be that his US connections were made then.

Billy certainly introduced Jack Johnson to the notorious gangster, racketeer and boxing promotor, Owney Madden: 'born in Leeds, raised in Wigan and King of the West Side'. Madden bought the nightclub premises owned by Jack Johnson and turned it into the famous Cotton Club. I don't know for sure, but I surmise that the connection between Madden and Billy was, of all things, pigeons. Billy was a keen pigeon fancier as was Madden, apparently. My aunt Janet told me that Billy used to send Madden copies of British pigeon flyers' magazines on a regular basis.

Going back to my London ancestors, I never actually knew these people. All I know is that for a while, they were the "muscle" for London gangsters and made infrequent visits north, George Lee and his brothers being part of their northern network. The only time I actually saw any of them was in about 1956.

I used to sit on the staircase behind a gate, where I could see everyone entering or leaving the pub, but I couldn't be seen. My father had been involved in a road accident and had cut his face quite badly. He was a bit knocked about but was still working behind the bar. One night, two men walked in. They looked like actors from *The Untouchables*, with double-breasted suits and fedora-type hats.

They spoke to my dad at the bottom of the stairs and even as a six year old, I thought that they had funny accents. They had heard my dad had been knocked about and wanted to know what was going on. He reassured them it had been an accident in his car, no one needed sorting out and all was okay. They were insistent that he let them know if there was a problem.

Fred would never discuss the connection: he was clearly determined not to be involved, and protected us from any association with the Londoners. My Aunt Janet did maintain a correspondence with this side of the family throughout the 60s and 70s and it was from her that I obtained what little information I have.

Fred was the eldest of George's five children: Janet, Steve, Bill and Margaret being his siblings. Steve was a Paratrooper who got badly injured and captured during Operation Market Garden when he jumped with a Polish battalion. On capture, after being treated by Polish medics, the Germans placed Steve in a hospital and took good care of him. However, they shot Steve's Polish comrades.

Fred was scrupulously honest, despising the activities of his father, keeping a distance between himself and the activities going on around him.

After being demobbed, Steve married the British nurse who had looked after him following his repatriation and went to live with her in Wales. He had little or no interaction with the rest of the Lee family after that. He became a senior librarian with, I believe, Cardiff library service. Like Fred, he despised his father's activities and would have nothing to do with criminal activity.

When I was six years old, my parents moved to the Dog and Partridge pub on Attercliffe Road where Fred and Joan had a successful run of four years, providing good beer, lively entertainment and a good night out seven nights per week. Few people had a TV in those days and the pub was an important central place for people to meet and socialize.

Like most pubs in the East End of Sheffield, it was rough. I used to sit on the stairs, obscured by a gate with peepholes in it, from where I could see the goings-on in the bar. On many occasions, I remember my dad slinging someone out. Fred loved a fight. One Saturday night, we had a wedding party in, a local Irish family: dozens of them. Two of the local "celebrities" came in and asked who was getting married. The name of the bride was revealed.

'Oh, I've shagged her,' one of them said.

The carnage went on for quite a while. When the police arrived, they waded in but they were losing for the first fifteen minutes. Fred couldn't stop laughing.

Fred was a complex character, naturally quiet as opposed to the bumptious and extrovert Joan. He was fastidious in the way he kept his cellar; there were areas near the barrels where only he could go. The saying 'you could eat your dinner off the floor' was literally true in Fred's cellar. He could be witty and funny. In drink, he became maudlin and unapproachable. If anyone came looking for trouble, they did not have to look far. He needed no bouncers, and many a "hard man" came looking for trouble, found it and didn't come back to look for any more. He loved violence, but at the same time, never sought it. When it kicked off, as it often did in the

East End of Sheffield in those days, Fred was in his element.

He killed a man. One night, a fight broke out in the large concert room and Fred went round, broke it up and escorted the trouble-maker to the door. As he did so, the man picked up a pint bottle and tried to strike Fred. The demolition was clinical: a left hook stunned the assailant and carried him to the door, a right hand had him going down and another left connected on the way down. As I write this, I can still hear the sound of the man's head hitting the concrete floor.

An ambulance came and the unconscious man was taken away. Later that evening, we learned the man had died. We also learned that he was a well-known thug with a reputation for using weapons, notably knives.

Nothing happened on the next day; then on the Sunday morning, two detectives from Attercliffe CID entered the tap room. I remember that my mother tried to busy herself, and that the customers stood silently as the cops ordered two halves of bitter. Fred served them. He asked if he was going to be arrested.

'No, not to worry,' the cop said. Then he said a sentence I will never forget. 'You keep knocking them down, Fred. We will scrape them up.'

We never heard another word about it. Hanging was the punishment for murder in these days; on reflection, Fred was a very lucky man.

Joan was the businessperson of the couple. If the pub was quiet, something was wrong. This was around the time that the music halls were closing and there were a number of old variety acts looking for work. The Dog and Partridge had a large concert room with a stage, and dressing rooms off to each side. "Turns" were booked: some comedians, an occasional magician but mostly singers: Toni Dalli, an Italian refugee, who went on to work in Las Vegas and made films in Italy, was a regular performer, as were Ronnie Dukes and Rikki Lee (no relation), who went on to do a Royal Variety Performance.

One day, I overheard Joan and Fred arguing. It transpired that she had booked a fan dancer, Lilly Marlene. Fred was outraged, but Joan was insistent that Lilly did not appear nude, but merely danced provocatively behind her fans. Fred gave in and the night arrived. I was told that Lilly had been very popular during the war. Looking at her, even as an eight year old, I wondered which war? Maybe the Boer.

Lilly did her number with the pianist and drummer positioned behind her. The pianist remained professional throughout the performance, but the drummer made faces and gesticulated to the crowd. At the end of her show, Lilly was to walk backwards to the rear of the stage, slowly opening her fans. As she was about to reveal herself, Fred was to turn all the house lights off, allowing her to leave the stage unseen. All went to plan and the house was in darkness.

Lilly dropped her fans and bent down to collect some items from the rear of the stage. As she did so, Fred, who had been drinking, turned the lights back on. Lilly panicked and, naked as the day she was born, ran towards the wrong dressing room. The crowd erupted as she turned, hands in appropriate places and ran across the stage to the correct room. By this time, the all-male crowd was hysterical and Fred was cheered to the roof tops.

At the end of the night, the last men to leave were two cops from the Licensing Department, who despite enjoying their evening, reported Fred for keeping a disorderly house.

He was fined 17/6 (about 80p). He nearly lost his license and there were headlines in the Sheffield Star newspaper. The offence boiled down to a middle-aged woman with no clothes on appearing on the stage for thirty seconds at most! As Fred had not wanted to hire Lilly in the first place, the atmosphere was a bit frosty in the Lee household.

It could be argued that amongst its achievements, the Lee family started the nearest thing we have ever had to a red light district in Sheffield, as Attercliffe later became the district where the massage parlours proliferated!

Joan was clearly an impressive landlady: big, blonde and buxom; she looked like Bet Lynch's older sister! Many years later as a young police officer, I locked up an Irishman we knew as Tipperary Tim, for being found drunk. Once he was sober, I was in the process of bailing him out and doing the paperwork. He noticed my name.

'Lee, is it? You have the look of that fine landlady from the Dog and Partridge on Attercliffe.'

I confirmed that she was my mother.

'Son, she had finer breasts than Jayne Mansfield,' was his sincere and respectful compliment. The police station went silent, awaiting my response. I thanked Tim and told him I would pass on his complements.

Joan was, and at ninety four, still is Joan: a true character, a good businesswoman and a good mother.

When I was ten years old, we moved to a pub in the centre of the steel producing area of Brightside, the Wellington on Brightside Lane. Incredible as it seems, most of the trade came from the men working in the hot steel works. At 11am when the pub opened, my parents, along with a couple of barmaids, worked flat out, filling empty "pop" bottles with draught beer, placing them into large satchels to be collected by the young lads and then distributed amongst the men on the forge floor.

The thought of men drinking several pints of beer midway through their shift would not, I believe, be acceptable to the Health and Safety-conscious management of today, but drink they did, and plenty of it. The big hammers in the forge operated day and night and the whole pub trembled when they struck.

Joan was responsible for building up the night-time trade from the equally nearby terraced houses and we soon had a regular piano player, sing-songs and an occasional paid "turn" to liven up the proceedings.

A boat trip in Bridlington with my dad.

A day out to Bakewell with Mum and Dad.

An outing with Joan's mum and dad.

Chapter 2: School Days and Growing Up

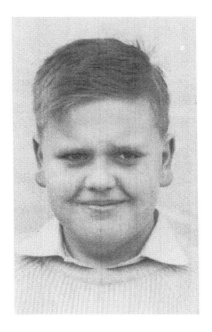

Me as a schoolboy.

All these changes of address meant that I moved schools quite often. At some point, when I was about eight years old, it was decided that I should go to a private school, which was in fact a "crammer", with the sole purpose of getting kids through the eleven plus. I hated the place. I hated the teachers and I didn't like the kids. I effectively switched off and was one of the few to fail the exam. In disgrace, I was sent to Hartley Brook Secondary Modern School in Shiregreen.

Most of the kids already knew each other and I was very much the outsider. Then I discovered rugby. Always big for my age, I was a natural prop forward and was soon playing in the under-thirteens team, despite being only eleven. I loved it: the engagement with sport, making good friends and generally enjoying life meant that my schoolwork improved and I was soon in the top class.

After a year, Joan and Fred decided to send me to another private school. Why they thought this was a good idea, I will never know. They sent me to Gregg, in Broomhill, in the leafy suburbs of Sheffield Ten.

Even after all these years, it is difficult to explain the depths of loathing I had for this place.

After a few weeks, I heard about a kid getting expelled. They didn't expel you at Hartley Brook, they just caned you. I now had a purpose in life, an ambition, a vision. I would get expelled.

I knew that soft core porn was available in a newsagent's shop near the pub: you could get anything down the "Cliffe". I learned that deliveries of newspapers and magazines were made in the early morning and were left for collection around the back of the shop.

I acquired several magazines, tame by today's standards but depraved by the standards of the genteel Sheffield Ten postcode. I placed the mags in various desks throughout the school. The result was electrifying: nervous girls and fascinated boys intermingled with outraged teachers, all apparently tearing about the place, desperately trying to find the perpetrator of this outrage. I left various clues but they were too thick to detect me. I eventually got kicked out after feigning a fit, frothing mouth and everything, and threatening to burn the place down.

Back to Hartley Brook, rugby and fun. I left without any qualifications. Most of my friends got apprenticeships. I had a few interviews but got nowhere, due to my complete lack of practical ability in anything. This, I feel, is due to the fact that my schooldays were ruined by chopping and changing schools.

My complete inability to be in any way "handy" has haunted me down the years. I can't paint, saw or turn a screw without disaster following. When anything needed fixing in the house, my lovely

Christine, a plumber's daughter, would step in. The kids referred to the case where the implements were stored as 'mum's toolbox'.

My parents had done well, and when I was fifteen, we moved again to another Wellington, this time the one at Darnall, still in Sheffield's East End but a more residential area, although the great companies of Davy United and Cravens were not far away. This pub was a gold mine and although I helped out most nights, I also got a job. My first job was working for the Coop as a van lad, delivering bread on the Parson Cross estate, and then later, I worked as a cellar man for a wine and spirit merchant, Porter Wright and Company.

As a van lad, I would deliver bread door-to-door on the Parson Cross estate. The driver would keep a record of what we had delivered and on Saturday mornings, we would go round and collect what was owed.

My boss, the van driver, was called Gordon. On the round we had several "cup of tea" stops. Some houses, I got invited into, others, Gordon went into alone. I soon realised that these stops were usually the homes of women whose husbands were at work. The visits used to last about thirty minutes and Gordon was always more relaxed when he got back on the van. I was worldly for my fifteen years and used to ask him if he had enjoyed his tea, clearly it was hot because he was sweating. Did he have any crumpets, etc.? Gordon had a great sense of humour and we would drive away laughing.

One day, Gordon told me that our sales of sweet goods: buns and cakes were down and we needed to do some selling. I would carry a large basket containing everything from malt loaves to teacakes from iced buns to French fancies. When I delivered the loaves, I would ask the customers to take a look in the basket to see if there was anything they liked. I was doing well and Gordon was pleased.

The most awkward customer was a woman called Mrs Murphy. She had one sliced loaf per day; that's all she ever had, and Gordon said there was no point in taking the basket, but take it I did. Mrs Murphy came to the door to collect her bread and I asked her if, when her husband came home from work that evening, the sight of a nice madeira cake or possibly a trio of buns would enhance his dining experience. (That was not what I actually said but you get the gist). She had a face similar to that of a Rottweiler that has been chewing a bee.

However, she said yes, called me a cheeky bleeder and snatched the cake. It went down on her tally. Gordon did not believe I had sold her the cake, told me there was no point in falsely inflating sales figures and that he was disappointed in me. I was quietly furious.

On the Saturday, when he not only collected her money but received a standing order for a weekly cake, he was delighted. Gordon apologised and shook my hand. I have negotiated some big contracts in my career, but still, my most satisfying sale was a cake to the difficult wife of a hard-working steelworker in 1963.

Occasionally in business meetings, I am asked who my business heroes are. I think I am expected to say Lord Sugar, Richard Branson and the like. Actually, my real business heroes are people like Gordon, who, day-in-day-out, deliver the goods, maintain the quality and cherish the brand.

My six months with Gordon was a defining experience in my career. He taught me to be honest, punctual, clean and tidy and respectful, and to value customers and take pride in myself. I don't think they teach you much more at Harvard. My business education started with Joan and Fred but was enhanced on the back of a bread van on the Parson Cross estate in Sheffield.

Porter Wright was another great experience. It's the sort of business that no longer exists, a retail wine and spirit merchant with its own line in whisky, gin and cigarettes. I never stole anything from there but I did borrow stuff now and again. They had some beautiful cigarette cases and lighters, and in the days when most people smoked, my fifteen and sixteen-year-old self could be seen in my three-piece suit, occasionally opening my gold-lined cigarette case and offering to light young ladies' cigarettes with my flash Ronson lighter. Monday morning's first job was to get the items back into the display case before anyone noticed!

Porter Wright's premises were in Castlegreen, just down from the Hen and Chickens pub and the Police station. The building was demolished to make way for the new courthouse, closing off the access to Lady's Bridge. The cellars were very deep and contained many thousands of pounds worth of vintage wines, port, sherry and a huge whisky store.

At one end of the cellar, which must have been fifteen feet high, was a bricked-up tunnel, easily wide enough for a coach and horses. The direction in which the tunnel pointed was towards Sheffield

Castle, the remains of which are now being closely examined by archaeologists due to the demolition of Castle Market. There has long been speculation about tunnels under Sheffield. When I asked about them, I was told that this was the tunnel through which visitors to Mary Queen of Scots visitors gained access to her. I have no doubt this tunnel existed and ran from the general direction of West Bar towards the Castle, passing under Castle Green.

The clientele at Porter Wright was rather posh when compared to the Coop, but there were some really nice regular customers, one of whom was a retired Royal Navy Commander. I was watching TV one Sunday afternoon at the time and a film came on, starring John Mills as a Royal Navy Commander with the same name as our customer.

The plot of the film was that Italian divers had placed limpet mines on a British warship. It was known that the mines were set to explode at 3pm. The divers were captured but would not disclose where the mines had been placed. The drama unfolded as Mills confronted the Italians, stating that they were all going to stay on the ship, and when it blew up, they would all die together. The ticking clock, the perspiration on the foreheads of the Italians contrasting with the stoic British stiff upper lip all added to the rising tension, eventually, as expected, the Italians cracked, the mines were found and all was well as the Union Jack flapped in the wind.

The next time the Commander visited us, I asked him if he was in fact the man portrayed in the film. He said he was. I then told him how much I admired his cool courage and tenacity in dealing with the cowardly Italians. He smiled ruefully and told me that it was not quite as it had been portrayed. He said that the Italians were in fact very brave men, but that at 2.30pm, they were tied to their chairs and told that the British were in fact going to abandon ship, leaving them to benefit fully from the explosion. It was under these circumstances that the Italians gave up the positions of the mines. I have no doubt the Commander was in fact a very brave man. I also learned he was not a fool.

I played rugby for a couple of years for Sheffield Tigers in Dore, although as an East End of Sheffield lad, I didn't really fit in with the posher kids from that side of the city and called it a day. I did a bit of boxing, but my size was such that I was a difficult lad to get matches for and I ended up boxing the same lads time and again.

About this time, I met the great Brendan Ingle, who has been a friend ever since. If, dear reader, you don't know the Irishman, you should make the effort to meet him. He is a truly remarkable man, who in his time has done more for community cohesion and racial equality than most politicians. And at the same time, he has created numerous boxing champions. Better writers than me have expounded on the life of Brendan. Please get to know more about him. You will be a better person for it.

I also tried my hand at amateur wrestling and joined a club situated over the Ball public house in Darnall. It was run by a Hungarian émigré called Joe (surname unpronounceable). He had represented Hungary in international competitions before the 1956 uprising. He weighed 9stone 2lbs. I remember this because I was exactly double his weight at 18stone 4lbs.

On my first visit to the club, he singled me out and got me to the centre of the mat. He beckoned me forward and I shrugged, thinking all I had to do was to push him over and sit on him. My next thought was that the ceiling needed painting as he threw me with consummate ease.

Amateur wrestling was and is very much a minority sport but I met some really good lads, many who remained friends for years. One was Tony, whose full-time job was as a bouncer at the Cavern in Liverpool. The place had been terrorized by thugs for years until he took over the door. When the place was turned into a museum, they erected a life-sized picture of him and placed it in the door: a tough guy but a lovely human being.

On Saturday mornings, Joe used to run a kids' session. He asked me to go and help him out. The problem was that the kids were strangling each other! His instruction was that if you placed your opponent in a headlock, the hold had to be placed on the line of the jaw, not across the wind pipe. The procedure was that if you were the recipient of this hold and your breathing was constricted, you should tap your opponent's arm and the referee would check that you were safe. 'Tap tap tap' was the phrase you heard most from Joe. Despite his entreaties, the kids continued to try to kill each other!

After another near-death experience, Joe got the lads together and told the following story. Try to imagine this in an East European accent and visualise this tiny man with no neck, just a knot of muscle with a head on it!

'Ven I escape from Budapest in 1956, I am hiding in a wardrobe with three other wrestlers, waiting for a truck to come to take us to Vienna. They are Tibor and Peter Zackass [both leading pro wrestlers and World of Sport favorites in the 60s and 70s], also Josef Kovacks [the "butcher of Budapest", weighing twenty-five stones and one of strongest men in world]. My sister looks out of window, keeping eye for transport. Down road come Russian soldier with gun and long bayonet, he sees sister and comes into room to rape her, he puts gun against wall and as he take hold of her, Kovacks comes out of wardrobe and takes him in stranglehold from behind, and he skveeeeeese, he lets Russian reach out and touch gun and then he skveeeeeeeze. It took Russian twenty minutes to die.' The kids' eyes were out on stalks by this time.

'Russian forgot to TAP'. There were no more issues with strangulation!

My parents' pub was booming and they asked me to help full time, so I packed up the job I loved at Porter Wright and joined the family business.

My parents, Fred and Joan, behind the bar of the Wellington in the 1960s.

Darnall was full of characters, mostly hard-working men in the engineering and steel works, a few scrap metal dealers, and a well-established gay community. It was all supplied by several big busy pubs, working men's clubs, a cinema and lots of small food retailers.

Next to the Wellington was Frank Peache's barbers, for a youngster like me, a hotbed of saucy men's magazines, although they were tame by today's standards. *Sporting Life* magazine had the horse racing tips, and while you were getting a haircut, you could listen to all the gossip about United and Wednesday. One day, one of the scrap dealers came in and told Frank he owned a horse that was running at Doncaster – it was a long shot but would be worth trying.

By the time Frank repeated the tale in the Wellington, it could not fail to win. Everyone had a bet, large and small, and it won, at fifty-to-one. The horse was called Supreme Sovereign. Rio has not had a celebration to compare to the one we had in Darnall that afternoon!

Frank's wife Margaret worked at the Northern General Hospital as a technician. They decided that it was time I had a date. On Wednesday evenings, I would travel to the centre of Sheffield to meet a young lady, for a date organised by Margaret, I found the experience somewhat traumatic. My interests, in rugby, boxing and bull terriers, were not particularly attractive to the refined young ladies I was introduced to.

After about six of these escapades, I think Frank and Margaret gave me up as a bad job. Actually, from my point of view, these weekly meetings were very productive. I did not realise it at the time but one of the ladies was the woman to whom I have had the honour of being married to for nearly fifty years, but more of that later.

Darnall was a great place to live in the 60s, and to me, the Wellington was the centre of it all. My first introduction to the local gay contingent was on the first night that Fred and Joan took the place over. Fred got me on one side and explained to me about these "puffs" (please excuse the terminology, but I am telling the story using the vernacular of the time). Fred explained that they were effeminate men who wore make up and that I was just to treat them as I would anyone else.

Although I was underage, I did serve if the bar staff got busy, and one night, I was confronted by a very large man in a flat cap, white muffler and eye shadow! Clearly a "puff".

He asked for a pint, I pulled it and placed it before him, avoiding eye contact. He downed the pint in one and handed it back to me, ordering a refill. This time, he quaffed half the beer and went off to join some other, more normal-looking men playing dominoes.

I pointed the man out to Fred, who immediately burst out laughing. He explained to me that the eye liner was coal dust; the man was a miner on his way home. He then pointed out an area of the pub forever called thereafter "puffs' corner". It was occupied by a few men with coiffed hair and makeup. Why I had not noticed this lot before and picked out the miner, I will never know.

The most prominent of the gay contingent was Ernest Morley. He was hysterically funny, with a line in repartee that any comedian would treasure; his outlandish appearance often completed by his poodle, whose hair he had dyed to match his own. Not many people have seen a blonde poodle with a blue rinse, but I have.

There was another side to Ernest, who was a male nurse at Weston Park cancer hospital. He was respected and dare I say loved by many, whose relatives he had nursed. One Saturday afternoon, a Mrs Critchlow, the wife of one of the area's toughest men and largest families went into premature labour whilst shopping in Darnall. Ernest took her into his pristine home, assisted her and brought a bouncing baby into the world to add to the vast Critchlow brood. This incident added to Ernest's credibility and he was accepted for what he was: outlandish, colourful and funny, but caring, kind and resourceful.

One Saturday night, the place was packed when a group of strangers entered. They got a drink and noticed the noise and gaiety emanating from "puffs' corner". They started to take the mickey, got verbally savaged by Ernest and it was about to get physical. Fred went over to the strangers and told them to leave. One of them asked if we were all "puffs" in this pub. In a big, booming voice, Big Joe Critchlow spoke for the Darnall community.

'As far as you are concerned, yes. We are all "puffs" in here.' The men left, quickly.

There was a large Polish contingent too. They were men who had escaped during the war and had made their homes in Sheffield, working in the pits and steelworks. Heavy drinkers, their night was Saturday. After numerous pints of English ale, they would end the evening by lining up at the bar and demanding Wisniowka, this being a strong cherry vodka. Fred had bought in several bottles and it became a tradition that he would line up a number of specially acquired "shot" type glasses and serve the Poles. They would then sing and empty the bottle.

They cried too. I found this a bit embarrassing and one night, I asked Fred why they got so upset.

'It's because they can't go home,' was his reply. I noticed a tear in his eye as well. Fred was very fond of the Poles and I later found that his brother, my uncle Steve, was attached to a Polish paratroop regiment in the Second World War. He had jumped with them during operation Market Garden, was wounded and tended by Polish medics until they were captured by Germans. As I mentioned earlier, apparently Steve was made a Prisoner of War, while the Germans shot the Poles.

Steve's affection and respect for his comrades was passed on by his older brother to these men, who were now our customers and who worked hard in the steel works and the mines of South Yorkshire.

There was a large family of African descent living near us. One of their sons became a leading sports trainer; another had been a POW in Japan in the Second World War. Their sister was a beauty queen. We talk today of the importance of integration, diversity and equality, but Darnall was a beacon of these aspirations in the 60s. The community was centred on the pubs and clubs, and to a lesser extent, the churches and chapels.

When the breweries priced the working man out of pubs, the artists priced themselves out of the clubs and immigration went unchecked, the nature of Darnall and other areas changed. We lost community cohesion and that integration as the older population felt swamped and squeezed. Thatcher then did what she did and the fundamental nature of work changed. I think we lost a lot.

Darnall had an interesting criminal fraternity. The steel works and supporting industries provided opportunities for metal thieves, as it still does. Other forms of criminality were always present and I soon got to know many of the men who made their living on the wrong side of the law.

The most prominent of them was a man I will call Tommy. Aged about thirty at the time, he drove a Bentley, wore bespoke suits, was friendly and funny but had a fearsome reputation as an "on the cobbles" fighting man. Interestingly, he always deferred to Fred. My dad's reputation was from an older generation, but Tommy never challenged it.

Tommy would start his nights out at the Wellington before moving on to other drinking haunts, where we heard stories about violent behaviour and criminal activity. In the Wellington, he was a perfect customer.

One of his associates was a man I will call Scobie. This was because of his liking for horseracing. He was a successful professional gambler. Unfortunately, he was riddled with arthritis and was usually in pain. His hands bent at the wrist and his fingers were twisted.

One day, Fred was out with Joan and I was in charge of the bar. Scobie was in alone, having a drink and studying form, when in walked three brothers. All well-known trouble makers, they were huge men, all above six feet tall.

As soon as they saw Scobie, they stared to pick on him. He tied them up in knots verbally, but as soon as it got physical, he was in deep trouble. I asked them to leave him alone and they just ignored me. One of them back-handed Scobie and I realised I had to act. In the back yard were our two bull terriers, Mac and Alma. I let them in and, to paraphrase Russell Crowe in Gladiator: 'on my command, hell was released'.

Mac took hold of Scobie's assailant's backside. Alma went for another one's groin. I expect not many dear readers have ever been bitten by a full-sized Bull Terrier. Think of a Great White Shark in miniature.

Scobie picked up a tray from the bar and began to beat away at the enemy. At this point, the "puffs" arrived. Ernest, accompanied by his "friend" Edgar, passed his pink poodle to a watching customer and dived in. By this time, I had got a barmaid to go and fetch Fred's mallet, which he used to tap the barrels. Suitably armed, I attacked. In a short time, the brothers were bloodied, bitten and in full retreat. I prised the dogs off them and they ran out, threatening retribution.

That night, I was working, when in walked Tommy and a coterie of Darnall's finest, including Scobie. All wearing three-piece-suits, gold watches and assorted bling. Fred and Joan were both behind the bar and knew what had happened but were a bit concerned about the deputation.

Tommy asked to see me and I went round the bar. He told me that as far as he and the rest of them were concerned, what I had done in rescuing Scobie was above and beyond the call of duty, that the brothers were dangerous and that most people would not have taken them on. And that if ever I needed help, I only had to call. I never paid to enter a nightclub or disco in Sheffield again. I didn't get into the full picture with Tommy, which included Ernest's gay tag team and the attack terriers, but as Scobie didn't mention it, neither did I!

One New Year's Eve night, Frank and Margaret held a party at their house behind the barbers. Margaret's friends and work mates were doctors, nurses and other professionals, not used to us rough East End types, but the party was going well. I was sat on a settee taking it all in, drinking brandy and Babycham (which was cool at the time)! Word got around that a well-known gangster was going to visit the party and there was a tangible tension when in walked Tommy. He got a drink, sat next to me and we were having a chat when I told him about the pending visit of a gangster. We kept glancing at the back door, expecting a James Cagney or Humphrey Bogart type to enter. I looked up and realised all the eyes in the room were on Tommy. Behind my hand I whispered:

'Tom, it's you.' He followed my gaze and seeing the effect he was having, raised his glass and wished everyone a happy new year. The tension eased and the party picked up again.

Tommy was quiet, respectful and good company. He was a villain, he was violent, but he never broke into anyone's house or clipped anyone who didn't come looking for trouble. I liked Tommy.

A night out at the Wellington.

When we closed the pub, I would jump into my Mark One Cortina and head for the fleshpots of Sheffield: The Cavendish, Penny Farthing and Heartbeat nightclubs were the places to be seen, and at least three times a week, I could be found propping up the bar.

I had few friends my own age, and those I had were courting or engaged. I knew the bouncers, the bar staff and a number of the city centre characters. I had been vouched for by Tommy and Scobie, and always felt at home.

One night in the Cavendish, I was watching the people on the dance floor when I felt a tap on my back. I turned and saw one of the young women I had been introduced to by Margaret and Frank. She was dressed in a blue mini-dress with white edging. She had short hair and brown eyes. I fell in love at that moment, and I'm in love with her still: the awkward, contrary, argumentative, brilliant, organised, fabulous Christine Joan Thompson. My first line was a real killer:

'Hello luv.' It was that good that I've repeated it every morning for the last fifty years.

Christine was working as a technician at the Northern Hospital, in the cardio department. Her boss was Dr Reg Saynor, a lovely guy, who went on to become a professor and a distinguished author and world-renowned researcher on heart disease. Had Christine continued working with Reg, she may well have achieved the same heights of achievement.

Instead, she eventually joined me on a journey that has included running "difficult" pubs and nightclubs, working during the Miners' Strike, evacuating Aintree racecourse, creating one of the most respected security companies in the country and having two great kids on the way.

I often look at Christine and wonder why she has stuck around. I cannot be the easiest person to live with! I like to think it is love that keeps us together, but in my darker moments, I think it may be curiosity, wondering and afraid to miss whatever scrape I am going to get us into next.

From the moment I met her, I knew I had to move on. The jobs I had had were menial, notwithstanding I always had access to cash.

I thought long and hard about my future and then I took a logical step for a young man whose grandfather was Sheffield's biggest receiver of stolen goods and whose own father was lucky not be hanged.

I joined the Police force.

Chapter 3: Boy in Blue

I did it all for her: cutting the cake with Christine at our wedding. She's

always been my inspiration and motivation.

Whilst waiting for my vetting to clear to join the police, I got a job with the London Brick Company as a lorry driver's mate, loading and unloading bricks by hand, onto and off large lorries. We did six loads a day: a total of 17,500 bricks every shift, and a total of 105,000 bricks per week, assuming a six-day week. It was back-breaking work, but well paid. I got fit and tanned through the summer of 1968, and also, I built up a tidy nest egg of cash.

This amount was enhanced on the Sunday before I was due to go to the police training school on Monday. I dropped Chris off at her parents' house and I went on a lonesome night out, visiting, maybe for the last time, many of my old city centre haunts. Obviously life was going to change for me and it was a fairly nostalgic visit to places and acquaintances I would not be seeing for a long time.

I bumped into Scobie. We talked and I explained that I had left the Wellington and my parents and had a new job starting "up north" from next week. I never told him it was at the police training centre! He asked me how I was fixed for cash and I told him I was okay. To cut a long story short, Scobie decided I needed some more and, after hailing a taxi, we ended up in a gambling den in the Attercliffe area, run by an ex-pro boxer. He sat at the table dealing blackjack.

Apparently the "pitch" was a 60s-style money laundering operation, the details of which I never asked. Scobie sat me at the table, taking the chair next to me. He nodded at the dealer and within half an hour, starting with £2, I had made £250. I guess that's about £5k in today's money.

We cashed in, left the gambling den and I never returned. Outside, I shook hands with Scobie and I could not bear to continue to lie to him. I told him what I was doing. He told me that he already knew, that he had known for a while and despite being surprised, he wished me well, that I was a good kid and he would never forget the battle in the tap room. I never saw Scobie for many years. He was a criminal, and a dangerous man, despite his physical limitations. He was also a friend of mine.

The first week in the cops was in a training room above the Black Swan pub on Scotland Street. We all trooped in, wearing our starchy new uniforms, and sat expectantly waiting for the instructor to enlighten us. He started by issuing a blue-coloured A4 paper sheet, containing ten face pictures and details of Sheffield's most active criminals. I was on first-name terms with about eight of them! Tommy was top of the list, Scobie about number five.

The cash from last night's gambling session seemed to turn warm in my pocket. The instructor then started on a long meandering load of waffle about how evil these men were, how we should treat them with utmost suspicion and how they were involved in major crimes. I never discovered what these crimes were. I can only assume they were never reported, or more likely, were the result of over-active imaginations by those within the police service who had difficulty justifying their own existence.

I never mentioned the fact that I knew this lot. I had been vetted and I had never been in trouble. Indeed, I had been raised in an environment that was very crime-averse. I kept my head down and tried to look impressed, but my first impression of the police was one of a naïve organisation, certainly at a training level.

When I got to the police training school, I realised how bad my paperwork was. I could spell, but after rather an itinerant childhood, changing schools as my parents changed pubs, my handwriting was terrible and my overall education was disjointed. Indeed, I was so terrible on paper, I really thought they were going to throw me out.

One day we were on parade with the drill instructor Bill Gledhill, who, on first impression, seemed an incarnation of the devil himself, but who was, when you got to know him, a kindly if no-nonsense type of man who, eventually, everyone liked and respected.

Bill was walking up and down the lines of young cops, asking them about themselves. He went up to one unfortunate and asked him what he did before training as a *policeman*. He leered this word as though no matter what the student achieved, he would never actually achieve the right to call himself a copper.

'Sales representative for Addis,' the lad replied.

'So what did you sell?'

'Brushes.'

'Brushes?' screamed Gledhill. 'You were a brush salesman?'

'Yes,' replied the hapless interviewee.

'Well say you are a fucking brush salesman then,' Gledhill screamed, his moustache bristling in a very brush-like manner.

Leaving the crestfallen former sales representative, he moved on. Anyone whose previous occupation showed any sign of pretentiousness was summarily demolished. Soldiers and sailors were okay. Then he got to me, and asked the standard question.

'Lorry driver's mate, sergeant.'

Gledhill stuck his face inches from mine.

'You will do, son,' he said, in a very quiet voice.

I got on well with Bill Gledhill. He realised my limitations, knew I was a trier and despite the obvious difficulty in me taking in the academic necessities, he encouraged and mentored me. I took no liberties, was respectful and listened and learned. He introduced me to another sergeant, Charlie Clarkson. Charlie was a genuine academic, more of a teacher than a copper. He gave me a piece of advice that I have always passed on to others who struggle with literacy.

'A newspaper a day, a magazine a week, a book a month. Read, and you will improve.' I did, and I have.

Every winter they held a novice boxing competition, and as I had boxed as an amateur to senior level, I was ineligible to take part. Training was under the direction of an old guy called Simmons, whose knowledge of boxing was more akin to John L Sullivan (who had his prime in the 1880s) than Mohammed Ali. All he succeeded in was getting the weaker of two men beaten up.

One night I went to the gym to watch them train and in walked Gledhill. He sat beside me and asked what I thought of the trainer. I told him exactly what I thought, and that I believed he was eventually going to get someone hurt. Gledhill thought for a bit and then asked me if I fancied training one squad and the Simmons the other. I immediately accepted and Simmons grudgingly agreed. He had first pick and I was left with a squad that, if Scobie had been around, I could have got long odds-on against winning.

Our opponents trained three times a week. So did we, but on the other nights, I had them in a small room out of sight and worked them hard. I taught them to jab and move, avoid infighting, and if in trouble, grab and hold until the referee broke them up. This was Brendan Ingle style, if not quality, training. We won the competition easily and even though I had a few losers, there wasn't much in it and no one got hurt or embarrassed. My star had risen.

Simmons stormed out and apparently, was never seen again. Gledhill hated the boxing instructor and subsequently, I could do no wrong.

My academic results were poor but Gledhill made sure that everyone knew I had put so much into the sporting and social field that my results were bound to suffer.

I graduated from the Police Training School with a glowing testimonial from Bill Gledhill. I look back with a great deal of gratitude to him, and I have tried to emulate him in the way I deal with the young, somewhat rootless youngsters in my own business: firm, no nonsense, but kind to people, usually young men, who are trying to get some stability and direction in their lives.

With Christine, I set up home in Brinsworth, Rotherham. This was convenient for me as I worked from Frederick Street, the HQ of G division of the then Sheffield and Rotherham Constabulary. However, this meant a couple of bus rides for Chris to the Northern General Hospital.

On my first day at Frederick Street, I reported for the afternoon shift, which was 2pm till 10pm. I was sent to the Inspector's office and met Inspector Jack Robbins and the Office Sergeant, Frank Scott.

I stood smartly to attention.

'After thirteen weeks in training school, do you know it all?' was the first question I was asked.

My answer was very honest: 'No Sir, I think I have a grounding but I guess my learning starts today.'

I saw Jack nod at Frank and realised that was a good answer. They were both ex-8th Army, tank men, who had seen battle, and after fighting Rommel, the local ne'er do wells did not impress these two. I quickly realised that these were the type of coppers I wanted to emulate.

I was sent out on the town centre beat with an experienced constable for about two weeks. In that time, we dealt with a few drunks, parking issues, lost kids and ambulance calls.

On my first day on my own, it was a 6am till 2pm day shift on Sunday morning. Inspector Robbins called me into his office. He told me to be careful, not to get too bothered about quoting the acts and sections relevant to implementing the law; that arresting someone for Drunk and Disorderly covered everything from bad parking to mass murder: just get the prisoner into the nick and he would sort the paperwork out.

Frank added to this by telling me to trust my judgment. If someone was doing something wrong, bring them to the police station, and there would be a law to cover it. This sounds very simplistic, but it actually gave you the confidence to do your job, knowing you had the backing of the experienced senior officers.

I had only been out a few minutes when I was sent to Doncaster Gate hospital and told to report to the sister in A&E. I got there and saw that the sister was bleeding from her mouth. She told me that a drunk who had been admitted the night before was now "kicking off". He had punched her and was now being threatening to other patients and female staff.

I asked if he was fit to be discharged and she said he was. At this point, I heard shouting and went to the ward. Behind drawn curtains I could hear female staff trying to calm the man, but he was verbally vile and lashing out at them. I opened the curtain. For the first time, I realised the power of my uniform. He lost his colour and froze to the spot.

I asked the nurses to leave and told him to put his clothes on. He started to tell me how ill he was and I told him that he was being taken into custody for special treatment.

'Where?' he asked.

'Cell eight, Frederick Street,' I replied. 'And if you think you're going to get violent, you really ought to control yourself, as I won't hesitate to flatten you.'

I took him in, and locked him up, but the nurse would not make a complaint, so no charges could be made. However, his card was marked. All the cops at the station were made aware of him and his activities. Every time he was seen in Rotherham town centre, he was spoken to and frankly, intimidated. Today it would be said that his human rights were compromised. Yes, they were, and I was delighted we did it.

Rotherham was a good place to learn how to be a cop. It was a small town, yet it had a murder rate three times higher than neighbouring Sheffield. There was a lively pub and club culture, with subsequent violent interactions once the licensed premises emptied. I soon found that my confidence in dealing with such matters made me a useful pair of hands when things "kicked off". Policing was a bit heavy-handed by today's standards and anyone looking for trouble would be swiftly accommodated.

As in any town, there were characters. One was Wally, an unfortunate man, whose background I did not know, but he should have been under some form of supervision. He made a living by collecting scrap metal. He worked very hard at it, but instead of renting somewhere to live, he spent his money on drink and dossed down in a stable. Wally was frequently in the cells for various drunkenness offences. He was a scary-looking bloke, but talked to properly, he would comply.

In the early hours of the morning of a freezing cold night, I was on foot patrol in the town centre, when I met the PC from an adjoining beat. He told me he had met Wally a few minutes earlier.

Apparently Wally had been kicked out of the stables and was looking for somewhere warm to sleep. He had asked the PC to lock him up so that he wouldn't freeze. The PC had explained to Wally that he couldn't lock him up as he hadn't done anything wrong. As a joke, he advised him to go and smash a few windows. The PC thought this was amusing. I wondered, and a few seconds later, we heard the sound of breaking glass as Wally commenced his destruction of the town centre shop windows. We got to him just as he was about to lob a brick at the huge plate glass window of a furniture store. Unfortunately, he had broken about six windows before we got to him and his first words to us as we got there were:

'Is that enough?'

We swore Wally to silence about the advice he had received from my colleague and we locked him up for Wilful Damage. He got three months. It was January: he would be out for spring, and he would be alive.

About a year later, I was on the morning shift and was assigned to the Masborough foot beat. It was another freezing morning and there was a thick pea-souper fog, the like of which you have to be over sixty years old to remember.

As I walked up Masborough Street, I found Wally sitting in a doorway, freezing. He had been kicked out of the stables again. He appeared pretty desperate and I took him to the small café a little further up the road. He was barred from entering the seating area, so I took him to a small outhouse at the rear, spoke to the owner and ordered him a bacon sandwich and a pint of hot tea, with the request that he allow Wally to remain there until the weather warmed up. I paid the owner and continued on my beat.

Next morning, I reported for work and was informed that I would be on cells duty. The Magistrates Court was attached to the Police Station and the job was to get the prisoners in and out of court, either back to the cells or released. I checked the list and there at the top of the list was Wally. I went to his cell and there he was, huddled up in the corner. He was charged with being Drunk and Disorderly.

Wally was the last prisoner to face the magistrates and I noticed that he was clearly embarrassed by my presence. Although I didn't speak to him, he was aware of my disappointment. We walked into the court and he took his place in the dock, with me standing behind him.

The charge was read out. It appeared that he had been in a pub in the Canklow area. The licensee wanted him out but he wouldn't go. Eventually the cops were called and he was ejected, but as he left, he had picked up a pint pot and hurled it at the mirror behind the bar, breaking it. The magistrate was Bill Owen, a bus driver by profession, a keen trade unionist and a thoroughly decent down-to-earth man.

He asked Wally for an explanation. It went something like this:

'Yesterday Morning I were a dying man – alone in the world, not even allowed to sleep wi' 'orses. It were freezing and I honestly thought my time was up, when out of the fog there emerged a giant, a caped hero, who offered me the hand of friendship, who provided me with money to buy food and a warm drink, who placed me in a warm room, and told that bastard at the Kenbet café to look after me till it had warmed up a bit. I took his money, ate the food and drank the tea. Then temptation got the better of me and I legged it before he came for the money. Later, I stole some lead from them derelict houses on Sarah Street and weighed it in for two quid. I started drinking then and were pissed up by night-time. Thee, Owen,' he said, indicating the Chairman of the Magistrates. 'Th'art nowt but a bus driver and I couldn't care less what tha sez but...' Wally then turned to me. 'I'm sorry, Mick,'.

I did not know where to look. The prosecuting police officer rolled his eyes and there was a good deal of paper shuffling. Then Mr Owen, ignoring the advice of the Clerk of the Court that I was not a sworn witness, asked me if I had some influence on Wally.

I stated that I had no more influence over him than anyone else but I took the opportunity to state that Wally was actually a hard-working bloke, with no support systems, no family or guidance. That when sober, he was eccentric, and when drunk, he was disruptive and a bit wild but in my opinion, not dangerous.

Mr Owen asked me what course of action I recommended. Remember, I was the gaoler, not a social worker – just a young PC with about two years' service. I advised him to imprison Wally until the spring: he would go to Leeds prison, where the governor would find him work, and he would be fed and housed. We could well be saving his life.

Bill Owen thought no more about it and sentenced him to three months. Anyone looking at Wally's record would think him an absolute nuisance. In fact, due to our society not being set up to deal with people like him, the cops and the magistrates conspired to get him sent to a place of safety. Albeit a few panes of glass and a pub mirror got damaged on the way.

After a while, I was promoted to the crime cars. This was a double-manned response vehicle, usually the first to arrive at any offence from shoplifters to fights: domestics through to murder. I enjoyed this aspect of the job and had some great partners, apart from one guy who had been kicked out of the CID and actually had a serious drink problem.

My first partner I will not name, because he went on to become one of the most respected Drug Squad officers in the country, working under cover and in serious danger much of the time. Society will never pay its debt to this man. He was responsible for the arrest of serious drug dealers all over the world. He remains a friend to this day.

When we worked together, we were locking people up faster than the CID could process them. We found informers amongst the youthful Rotherham criminal fraternity and worked them. In weeks, we had numerous arrests, and dozens of crimes, old and new, were cleared up. After a few weeks, my partner was moved on to the Plain Clothes department, the first step into a brilliant CID career.

His replacement was Roy. He was older than me, a serial womaniser, a heavy drinker and a comedian, and he had been a cop for over ten years. Caught fornicating on duty, he had been sentenced to the Rotherham Police version of Siberia and had been forgotten about for years, indeed for most of his service. I dreaded the thought of working with him as

I considered him idle. All I wanted to do was catch thieves, and I thought that all he wanted to do was mess about.

I was wrong. The first thing he said to me was:

'You've heard all about me. It's all true, but I've grown up and I want to work with you.'

He was a revelation: first on the scene at a fight, or a crime of any kind, Roy was first out of the car and into the middle of it. If it was likely to get violent, Roy had the habit of donning his skin-tight leather gloves. We cleared a few pubs in our time together.

These were times in which lawbreakers did not tend to complain if they received rough handling. Basically, if they behaved themselves and complied, they were well-treated; if they decided they wanted to fight or make life awkward, we responded in kind. Backed up by magistrates and senior officers, the streets of Rotherham were safe and the public were protected.

One Sunday afternoon, we received a call to go to a house in the Canklow district; a rough area by any standard, but an area whose populace I came to respect and like as time went by: straight-talking and honest (in their own way); they did not call a spade a shovel.

On arrival, we met an old lady who explained that in the house next door, there lived three Asian men, but recently, an African girl had moved in and our informant had heard her crying through the partition wall. We entered the lady's house and went upstairs, and listening, heard the clearly distressed voice of a woman and the guttural threatening tones of a man. A door slammed, and the sobs became louder as the woman was left alone.

We went to the house next door, knocked and the door opened a couple of inches. I asked where the young woman was who lived there. The face at the door replied that it was nothing to do with us; they knew their rights and there was no way we were coming in, and he slammed the door shut.

I turned to see Roy pulling his gloves on. Now legally, you need a warrant. We should have reported back to senior officers, written a report, and done all the timewasting bullshit that pervades modern policing.

We kicked the door open. Roy waded into the two men facing us. I went upstairs, following a middle-aged Asian man, who was clearly trying to get to the young woman before us.

I seized his belt from the rear and as he reached the landing, and used his own momentum to run him into the bathroom where he "fell" onto the sink. This caused an injury to his nose and mouth, and he decided to lie down and take a rest.

I went into the room containing the young woman. She was sat on the bed rocking to and fro, clearly traumatised. She was wearing traditional African dress with a turban and a long frock.

It later transpired she was Nigerian, a member of the Igbo tribe, who had fought against the government of General Yakubu Gowon in that country's bitter civil war. Her parents were dead, so she had made her own way to the UK and had somehow fallen into the clutches of the unconscious guy in the bathroom and his two mates currently being terrorised downstairs.

I asked her if she had been assaulted or in any way abused, and she said that she had. I asked her to come with me to the car. As she left the room, the last thing she picked up was her Bible.

I summoned another car and asked for a policewoman to attend. Within a few minutes, it arrived and after explaining the situation, the African lass was taken to Frederick Street.

I went back into the house, where Roy was towering over the settee, accommodating two cowering terrified liberty-takers who now realised that their feeling of invincibility was false. We cuffed them both, informing them they were under arrest for something – the details of which we would sort out later. They were clearly relieved to be in the back of another police car, and away from the gloved assassin.

At Frederick Street police station, the African lass was accommodated in the charge office, with copious cups of tea and jam sandwiches, while we waited for

Social Services to arrive. Social Services assisted the young woman, who eventually took up her education locally and went on to become a teacher, working in Rotherham for some years in the Canklow area. I saw her sometimes when we were driving about the town. She always waved, and she had a beautiful smile. If I ever achieved anything in my life, it was saving this young woman from the clutches of vile abusive men. Eventually, she went to live in the North East, married and had a family of her own.

If you were wondering what happened to the abusers, there was not enough evidence to convict them of sexual offences, nor, given the bumps, bruises, contusions, lost teeth and broken noses, was it considered a good idea to charge them with anything else. What I do know is that our efforts were appreciated in Canklow.

A few days later, Roy and I were on patrol when we were directed to a pub on Westgate where there was a fight. When we entered, the fight was still going on and we assisted the landlord in stopping it. Into the room came a well-known Canklow matriarch, who basically told the room to knock it off, as these were the two coppers who had got the "black lass" sorted out and that any more difficulty caused to us would be dealt with by her.

As I said earlier, Canklow was rough, but they looked after their own, and the "black lass" was, and stayed for some years, "one of their own".

When I read of the child exploitation scandal in Rotherham in recent years, I am appalled at the way police and social services failed in their responsibilities, as the liberal, multicultural imperative that started to gain purchase as I was leaving the police took hold. The result was that there was a serious failure in looking after the weak and vulnerable.

As police officers, we were far from perfect: rough, and sometimes brutal, but we weren't scared to get stuck in, take chances and make sure that those who needed help got it, even if we had to make things fit if we went to court.

Most of the cops I worked with were honest, conscientious men (and a few women too). There were some time-serving wasters, and some were daft, and just a very few were bent.

From time to time, I got sent to help out with the Regional Crime Squad. Usually, this involved staking out a property that was going to be burgled. We would be briefed by RCS officers and told that during the operation, the informer would be part of the gang attacking the property and that he would be allowed to escape.

The first time this happened, the informer turned out to be a well-known South Yorkshire crook, while those arrested were petty offenders of low intelligence and, during the time I spent with them, I realised that they had clearly been influenced to commit the crime by the informer. I soon realised that there was a conspiracy between the RCS and informers to "prop" crime, allowing the informer to commit crime unmolested as long as they supplied patsies to make the crime figures look good. It stank to high heaven and I told them so.

I was no longer invited to assist RCS. I was removed from the job I loved on the Crime Car and placed on a panda car beat. Many would have sulked, but I did my job, and not a day went by where I was not involved in some incident or other.

One night shift, I was asked to attend a suspected break-in at a tobacconist's shop in the Ferham area. On arrival, I saw a man in the shop stealing cigarettes and I arrested him. I took him to Frederick Street, processed him and placed him in the cells. I immediately suspected that this guy was different: he was quiet and well-dressed, not like the typical scroat you would expect to be turning over the local tobacconist.

Instantaneous access to computer records was not available in those days and it would be the next morning before I could check his true identity with the criminal records office. I suspected that this was a man worth knowing about. The prisoner was safely locked up, so I was happy to wait until the CID came on duty the following morning.

CID quickly established that the man, let's call him Larry, was a well-known professional crook, originating from London, but who had lived in various parts of the country before deciding to grace Rotherham with his presence. We got his address and searched the house where he was living. We found an Aladdin's cave of stolen property emanating from housebreakings in the Whirlow area of Sheffield, including gold, silver and jewellery worth many thousands of pounds. My instinct had proved right and we had a really good catch.

Larry was re-interviewed, was very open about his activities and made a full confession. He then asked to see officers from the RCS. At this point, after a straight twenty-four hours working, I left for some well-earned sleep.

I returned for duty at 10pm, to be met by the CID officers who had dealt with Larry throughout the time I had been absent. I asked how things were going. They were clearly infuriated and told me that he'd had a meeting with the RCS, during which he had offered to provide information on a top criminal on the basis that the charges against him would be dropped. It turned out that, in fact, he was to set up this criminal by offering to sell him the valuables from the burglaries that he, Larry, had committed.

In other words, this "top criminal" was not actually being investigated for reported crimes: he was to be set up. Larry had been bailed.

Larry was to contact the mark by phone and arrange to meet him near Norfolk Bridge not far from Sheffield city centre, at noon the following day.

It turned out that the "top criminal" was Tommy, my old friend from Darnall. A word of clarification here. If Tommy had committed criminal offences and I knew about it, I would have arrested him without hesitation. I took my oath seriously; I would administer the law without fear or favour, but the fact was that Tommy's convictions were all to do with violence, and those incidents had been perpetrated on those of his own kind.

No doubt Tommy was involved in high value metal fiddles, but none of this was reported crime. He merely exploited and benefitted from fiddles that had gone on for years and to an extent, still go on today in the steel industry. He was not a persistent post office robber, he did not blow safes or rob pensioners; he did not run protection rackets or drugs. These were the types of offences and offenders that the RCS should have been investigating. Instead, they went to their default position: they tried to fit him up.

I left the police station and drove to a phone box. I found Tommy's phone number and called him. A youngster answered and I asked to speak to Tommy.

'Who is it?' asked the young man.

'It's his cousin Frank,' I answered.

Tommy came on the phone. I outlined the fact that he was being set up, and told him not to turn up at Norfolk Bridge. He asked who I was. He seemed bemused as he did not recognise my voice. I did not tell him and then I hung up.

A few days later, I reported for duty and saw from the intelligence bulletin that Larry had been the victim of a robbery near his home; that he had sustained serious injuries, including broken ribs, lacerations and other injuries, none of them life-threatening but somewhat over the top, considering the low value of the money that had been stolen from him. Enquiries were made and interviews of known criminals took place. Regrettably, the crime went undetected. Larry relocated back to London shortly afterwards.

Years later, I was in a bar when Tommy came in as usual with a retinue. I acknowledged him over the bar and he came round to me. We had a drink, and he asked after Fred and Joan. Before leaving me, he shook hands.

'Look after yourself…Frank,' he said.

That was the last time we spoke to each other. He went on to become completely legitimate, with a number of successful businesses and a fine family, all of whom he kept well clear of criminality.

I continued to do my job but was becoming disillusioned. The RCS incidents had sickened me. I had aspired to join the CID but I now doubted whether it was a direction I wanted to take. Then the first stages of doubting whether or not I wanted to remain in the job at all started to emerge. The old guard of supervisory officers were fading away. Jack Robbins retired, as did a couple of the old sergeants. Their replacements were not of the same standard: this was the start of the careerists; those they replaced had been content to operate at Sergeant and Inspector level, serving the community and training and mentoring the constables under them.

The new lot were generally seeking promotion, keeping their noses clean and joining the right lodges.

This period also brought in the Bramshill boys, highly educated people who had passed through the National Police College in Hampshire, and were recruited on the basis that they would serve two years on the beat, then would automatically be promoted to the rank of Inspector.

We got one of them. In his two years on the beat, he had never made an arrest. His abilities seemed to be keeping his desk tidy and his uniform smart. After a few days, I started to wonder how he managed to cross the street unaided.

Two incidents made my mind up for me. One night, when I was sent from one side of the borough to the other to deal with a well-known hard case, and on the way there, I drove past several other coppers driving in the opposite direction, including the

Bramshill boy Inspector, each being paid as much and in his case, a lot more than me.

The other incident was when I was instructed to report to the Plain Clothes department for a six month assignment, prior to joining CID. On the morning, I was supposed to commence my Plain Clothes work, I was phoned and instructed not to bother and to return to normal duties. Not a word of explanation. I never asked for one. I left.

My leaving interview was with the Chief Constable of the time, Sir Philip Knights. He was not at Sheffield and Rotherham very long before going on to a very successful career in the West Midlands. His parting comment to me with my file in front of him was:

'I suspect you have been badly managed, young man. If you ever change your mind and want to come back to the service, find out where I am and contact me.'

It was nice to know that at least I was valued at a high level. I never took Sir Philip up on his offer. Nonetheless, I appreciated it.

Chapter 4: Adventures in the Pub Trade

Marti Caine opens the Mulberry Tavern in 1976.

After deciding to leave the police, I discussed the situation with my parents for ideas about my future career. I felt that perhaps it was time that I followed in their footsteps and became my own boss. Fred and Joan mentioned a few pubs that were on the market. Christine was keen to join me in my new venture.

Together, we looked at a few pubs, and found one that we thought we could make something of. Christine left her job in the NHS and we took on the Greengate Inn at High Green, at the north edge of Sheffield.

We were young and naive, but were keen to do a good job. The Greengate had been a difficult pub, with about twenty licensees in fifteen years. Big dirty discos had led to big nasty fights, and the place had developed a bad reputation.

The concert room had been closed for some time. Shotgun pellets fired by the last licensee still pebbled the ceiling. However, there was clearly a desire from the customers to restart the disco. We acquiesced, and for the first two Saturdays, we were fine. On the third week, we had a riot on our hands, and decided to do something drastic to alter the tone of the place.

The big band of the time was Roxy Music, who had a quite a sophisticated image. We replaced the old bar staff with young staff, all dressed in white à la Brian Ferry. Christine and the other barmaids dressed up in ankle-length dresses which were in fashion at the time.

We smartened up the room to make it look a bit more "cool" and installed the pub football team on the door, charging about ten pence per head (ladies free), with all monies going to the football club funds after the disco operator had been paid.

It worked well. The next week, ladies started to attend in smart dresses; the men smartened themselves up too – and we were in business.

We had been at the Greengate for a few months when I received an unexpected visit from a former senior police officer whom I had known only slightly during my time in the force. He called on me one morning as I opened the pub and as it was a quiet time, we sat and had a cup of tea together. The usual small talk ensued, during which he asked me if I had settled into my new lifestyle. After a while, he turned to me.

'If you were called on, would you serve again?' he said.

I was surprised at this, thinking he was encouraging me to re-join the Police Service.

Far from it. He informed me that he was now working in an intelligence role and that, from time to time, he needed to use personnel on a self-employed basis, to carry out certain low-key tasks involving transport, escort and security.

He told me that the pay was good but the work was irregular. I offered him my services. Over the next few years, I assisted at safe houses where Eastern Europeans and other persons were accommodated. I was never involved in any meaningful conversations with them but did, on occasion, escort these people on shopping trips, and from airports and military establishments.

The money was good. I was paid in cash, supplementing our pub income, and it led to some very good nights out. Christine was obviously aware of my sudden disappearances, which never lasted more than a couple of days, but she never complained or commented.

I started to do a fairly regular late night run to Runcorn in Cheshire. This would happen after we closed the pub, usually on a Friday night.

I would report to the ICI plant at Runcorn, get waved past the gatehouse and wait near the helicopter pad. Eventually a Sea King helicopter would fly in from the west, and it deposited a single passenger, whom I would then convey to a house in the Ranmoor district of Sheffield.

I was instructed not to enter into conversation with these passengers but you did not have to be a great investigator to realize that these men were Irish.

I would usually be required to reverse the journey on Sunday nights. I soon realised that these were persons of influence within political organisations who were attending discussions with what I assumed, quite wrongly, were British government contacts. I have often asked myself why the long trip from Runcorn to Sheffield was necessary, when a meeting in Liverpool or Manchester made more sense. The only answer is that I have no idea. I did the job and got paid.

The house at Ranmoor was ostensibly owned by British Steel. I handed my passengers over to a number of people, including a couple of Canadians. Over time, I got to know these people and would stop for a coffee and pass the time of night, before returning home to my pub on a rough council estate at the edge of Sheffield.

One of the Canadians was among the most remarkable physical specimens I have ever seen. Known as Big Pete, he was of French Canadian ancestry, born and brought up in Ottawa. He stood 6.8 inches tall and was a toned 300lbs.

At eighteen years old, he had wanted to immigrate to the USA, and found that if he served a period of three years in the US military, he was entitled to a green card. He joined the US Marine Corps. After completing the required time, he left the Marines and joined the Los Angeles Police Department. Big Pete had worked the tough streets of Watts and other notorious areas, earning a reputation as a no-nonsense individual. He moonlighted as a security man and bodyguard, numbering Marilyn Monroe and Howard Hughes amongst his clientele.

Big Pete was to play an important part in another chapter of my life, which I will come to later.

We enjoyed running the Greengate, but after a few years, it was time to move on and we were offered the Mulberry Tavern in Sheffield City Centre. We put our notice in, but as we were about to leave the Greengate, we were informed by the brewery that there was to be a six month delay in opening the new Mulberry Tavern.

We had no kids at the time and on reflection, maybe we should have taken some time out and gone travelling. We were only twenty-eight and twenty-nine, and could have enjoyed some freedom while we had the chance.

Instead, we took a short-term job managing a hotel-disco in Derbyshire. We did not start work until 10pm and I took the opportunity to get fit. I had piled weight on at the Greengate and felt very uncomfortable. We moved to Derbyshire in March, and the following summer of 1976 was one of the hottest on record. My diet and exercise regime bore fruit and during that summer, I lost about eight stones.

When November came and the Mulberry was ready, we were fit and ready to go. Marti Caine, the late-lamented comedienne and entertainer, opened the pub on 6th November 1976.

The brewery said they expected the place to take about £1,500 per week (a pint of beer in those days was about 25p!) We never took less than £4,000 per week, and that was when there was about three feet of snow on the ground! We averaged about £6,000 in wet sales only. The equivalent in 2017 would be about £60,000. That's an incredible amount for what was actually quite a small place.

The only problem was the brewery management: they were an odd mixture of drunks and incompetents. At the Greengate, we'd had a hands-off type of management, who just wanted you to sell their products and pay your bills. This lot were different, and were possibly the victims of too many management training courses.

The brewery carried out monthly stock-takes. The results were always acceptable but I worried that we only had the word of the stock-taker regarding its actual accuracy. One night, our Area Manager arrived, already half-cut and seeking to drink after the bar had closed. I was okay with this and indulged him. The next night, he was back, again drunk; again seeking to stay long into the early hours. This time, he was pawing the barmaids.

I eventually poured him into a taxi and sent him home. The next morning, I phoned him and told him to stay away from the pub when he was drunk. A week later, we had a stock-take. It showed a massive deficit. I suspected it was an act of revenge for me refusing to indulge the Area Manager. Clearly, he had got to the stock-takers and I was being set up.

They reckoned without Christine. Summoned to the brewery HQ, we delayed for a few hours and did our own stock check. Chris worked it out in minutes and we were actually in a slight surplus.

I went to the brewery alone, and into the Managing Director's office. He was a graduate, with all the arrogance of academia has when it's not backed up by practical experience. With him were the head stock-taker and the Area Manager. Their results were produced and I was asked for an explanation; clearly I was to be brought to book and told to toe the line.

Clearly, they expected me to grovel a bit, but I took out my own figures and showed my results. The Area Manager and head stock-taker blanched. I offered to go back with them to the pub and carry out another full check there and then. There was some blustering and I told the Managing Director that as far as I was concerned, I was the victim of a criminal conspiracy. He asked me to leave the office, and I never had any more issues with drunken brewery managers or bent stock-takers again. Bass were a shockingly bad employer; they thought that every employee was on the take, when actually the corruption was higher up.

In January 1980, the British Steel strike commenced and our pub takings plummeted. We received a visit from one of the board of directors from Bass, accompanied by the toadying local management. The director seemed a nice City type, with a striped suit and an old school tie.

'How's business?' he asked.

'In the middle of a steel strike, with the Thatcher government bent on destroying the unions and manufacturing, how could it be otherwise than poor?' I told him.

'I know the Sheffield people – they will always find the price of a pint', he replied.

My reply confirmed my "awkward" reputation at the brewery. I told him that the days when steelworkers coming home to eat their tea with nothing to cover the table other than last night's Star Newspaper were gone. The days of urchins waiting at pub doors for their dads to come out before they could eat were also over. I told him that people's aspirations nowadays included a mortgage, a car and a foreign holiday. Beer was actually quite a long way down the list. He was shocked, but he did listen.

One day, I was behind the bar when in walked a familiar giant. It was my old Canadian friend Big Pete. I never asked who Pete actually worked for, nor in fact did I ever ask who I was working for: my contact, the ex-senior cop sent me my instructions, paid me and left me alone until next time. Unfortunately in the months after we left the Greengate, my contact had a huge heart attack and died. I had thought at first that I was working for MI5, or some part of the government intelligence community. I wasn't.

Pete asked if we could talk alone. As it happened, Chris was away visiting her mother for the day, and when we closed the bar and everyone had left, Pete and I sat and talked. He told me that he and my former handler worked for some "leading businessmen", concerned initially about the Irish terrorist situation but who were now turning their attention to the rise in union power in the UK.

It turned out that I had provided the chauffeur service to and from Runcorn, to men whom these "businessmen" wanted to meet with covertly, to seek ways of ending the troubles. This initiative had clearly failed. Now they needed people within the union organisations to monitor what was going on and keep an eye on those left wing activists who were apparently determined to wreck the country.

All Big Pete wanted me to do was to keep in touch with him, allow him to count me as an ally, and wait. In subsequent years, I have discovered that the businessmen he represented were in fact, the remnants of an organisation called Great Britain 75, an organisation founded by David Stirling, founder of the SAS, set up to counter any revolutionary activity that may have emanated from ultra-left-wing activists.

GB75 had been infiltrated and undermined, but by the time Pete and I resumed our association, Stirling had reformed the organisation, backed by James Goldsmith, and was active in planting "moles" throughout the Trade Union movement.

Pete said that there was a possibility of a coup against the Wilson government, and that if it happened, trade union leaders and labour activists would be interred, and that Hillsborough, home of Sheffield Wednesday FC, would be used as a holding pen. He added that the army and police would round up the prisoners but that a team of people would need to be deployed to provide a warden-type service. Would I be part of it?

Frankly, I had trouble taking all of this in. I was now party to treason if the story was true: had this come from anyone else but Pete, I would have laughed and told them not to be stupid. The British Army would never be involved in a coup; this was the UK, not some banana republic. As it was, I did not believe it but I kept quiet.

When he had gone, I wondered what to do. The people I would have passed the info onto might be implicated. As the day wore on, I became more convinced that Pete was either winding me up or had gone mad. I finally convinced myself that what he had outlined was impossible in this country.

Two days later, the army took over Heathrow airport.

It has subsequently been explained that this "exercise" was to show the IRA that any move by them to attack Heathrow or elsewhere, would be swiftly thwarted. The facts that the IRA had never carried out such an attack previously and that the government were unaware of the army's actions were played down. I was told later that this action was designed to show the Wilson Government that unless things changed, there would be a coup.

Many years later, I was watching a TV programme about this period, and Roy Hattersley, the former Labour Home Secretary, was interviewed about the coup rumours. He was non-committal about whether he believed it but he was clear in stating that Wilson did. He cited an incident when Field Marshal Carver visited Downing Street for a scheduled meeting. Hattersley was used to the Field Marshal arriving in plain clothes. However, on this occasion, he arrived in full uniform. Hattersley said that Wilson nudged him and said: 'this is it', meaning that the coup was underway. It transpired that Field Marshal Carver had ceremonial responsibilities following the meeting and that Wilson was wrong.

Without displaying any enthusiasm, I told Pete that he could count on me. In the back of my mind, I did wonder what would have happened if I had turned him down, but my loyalties were clear in my own mind. The Trade Unions had gone mad; the red flag flew on Sheffield Town Hall, and if it was not yet time to stand up and be counted, it was a time for remaining quiet but prepared.

Nothing happened. The Labour party spluttered on, Prime Minister Wilson resigned; the Trade Unions continued a destructive path, and then in 1979, Margaret Thatcher was voted in. Throughout this period, I saw Pete a few times. I was still doing a little sporadic security/bodyguard work, but was more interested in running the pub.

We had done really well. Sheffield was a boom town in the mid to late 70s, with plenty of money and the mind-set to spend it. Sheffield's night-time economy was brilliant. Stars appeared at The Fiesta and there was World Championship Snooker at the Crucible.

Boxing became very popular, with Herol Graham, Mick Mills and Chris Walker fighting for titles at the Top rank or the City Hall. Josephine's nightclub was immensely popular; its owner the great Dave Allen setting a level of sophistication seldom seen in the North of England.

In 1979, under Thatcher, things started to change. A steel strike and redundancies caused a mood of pessimism and trade started to slip.

The brewery, badly managed and led, started to make cuts to staff and other economies that made life difficult. Service was poor and the downward spiral started. Renovations ceased. The place started to look shoddy. I got caught in a long-running dispute with the brewery and Chris and I started to feel that it was time we moved on.

One of our regulars was the local Woolworth's manager. One Saturday afternoon, he called in, as usual, for a sandwich and a pint.

I noticed that in addition, he was drinking brandy, in large amounts. He looked troubled and I went over and asked if he was ok. He explained that he was scared to go back to the store as, every Saturday for the past few weeks, a large group of West Indian youths had come into the store at about 4pm, taken over the cafeteria and were causing mayhem. The police were fed up with attending and were useless anyway.

At the Mulberry Tavern, we had recruited many of Brendan Ingle's boxes as barmen. They were fit young men, non-drinkers, with the excellent communication and social skills that Brendan had taught them. They included Herol Graham, Peter Bennett and the Vahey brothers, Vinnie and Vincent. I offered our services.

When we locked up the pub for the afternoon, all five of us went for a coffee in the Woolworth's cafeteria, and, as we had been warned, the place was full of disaffected West Indian black youths causing trouble. When we entered and the youths saw that Bomber Graham had come to call, it was like the Wild West saloon when the piano stops playing.

We soon kicked the appropriate backside, outed the whole bunch of them and prepared to leave. As we did so, the manager approached us, accompanied by a rotund gentleman with a very red face, who turned out to be the Area Manager. He was clearly impressed by what he had seen.

He was even more impressed when one of the barmen spotted a shoplifter. He asked me if we did this kind of thing anywhere else. When I explained I was the manager of a nearby pub, he was somewhat deflated, explaining that he had these kind of problems in other stores throughout the north of England.

I took his card, shook hands and went back to the Mulberry.

That evening, the weather was sultry, hot and sweaty, far too warm to be working. The doors to the pub were open and the fans were all on, when in walked a weird-looking guy, stripped to the waist and covered in hand-done tattoos. He was obviously under the influence of something, but before I could get to him to refuse him service, one of the barmaids had served him and he promptly set about indecently assaulting female customers, I went around the bar and took hold of him to throw him out, but he wanted to struggle a bit so I subdued him and sent for the cops, who came and took him away in their van. Nothing special; just another night in the city centre.

I washed my hands and went back behind the bar. A few minutes later, the police were on the phone and I took the call from an Inspector from West Bar Police Station. He informed me that the prisoner I had just handed over to them was well-known to them, and that he had a rare form of hepatitis that was very infectious. They told me that I was to hang up the phone and take a call from the hospital. I placed the phone down, quaking with fear. Chris was upstairs in the flat with our two infant kids. What had I done?

The phone went again. It was a sister from the hospital. I was to bag all my clothes and stand under a hot shower. She said that they were on the way to collect me. I was whisked off to the hospital. Blood, urine and saliva tests were taken, and I was strictly instructed to stay away from my wife and the kids. I was not to work.

I dispatched Chris and the kids to our house in Stannington, and remained in the flat, while staff ran the pub. I informed the brewery about what had happened and asked if they had any instructions, and I received none.

Nor did anyone call or contact me from the brewery. Four weeks later, I received the all-clear from the NHS. I had lost two stones through worrying. Chris and the kids returned and life seemed really good again.

Then the brewery came to call. The Director told me how concerned they were. I thanked him for his concern, and he asked me how this sort of thing could happen. I replied that these things are sent to try us. After a few meaningless exchanges of this type, I realised we were at cross purposes. I thought he was there as a concerned employer, offering commiserations for my recent ordeal. He wasn't. The stock check had revealed a £12 loss over a four-week period, against takings of over £20,000.

It would have been easy to walk out. Instead, the following Monday, I phoned Woolworth's and spoke to the gentleman I had met some weeks before. I was immediately offered contracts At Wakefield, Leeds, and Sheffield.

We met again; we arranged a rollout of other stores and within a month, we were servicing about twelve Woolworth's shops.

Word got round and we were contacted by the Coop, who had trouble in their Leo's Stores in Grimsby and Scunthorpe. Later, the Pennywise group called us, among many others.

As 1980 drew to a close, we had established a good, profitable business. Still we carried on at the Mulberry. In our hearts, we thought that a change of management at the brewery might bring along someone with half a brain, but by August 1981, we'd had enough and quit.

We had a house in the Stannington area of Sheffield and now with two kids, settled down to a new career and change of pace. Even then, the Bass management could not let you go without an attempt to besmirch your character. Word went round that we had been sacked, and that when we left the flat, it had to be fumigated – all lies.

I was clearly very much disliked at the brewery. I had exposed their corruption, and at the same time, run a highly-successful establishment, taking far more money than they had ever believed possible, with no doormen, no stock deficiencies that they hadn't made up, for a company that was corrupt from top to bottom, which held its employees in contempt and was so distant from its customers that it eventually lost them, and the Mulberry, an absolute cash cow, closed as did so many others. My only regret is that I never sued them. However, that chapter was closed

and the security business beckoned.

Chapter 5: Darth Vader's Minder

Johnny Nelson, one of six future world boxing champions who have worked with me at Constant Security.

When I started out in the security business, it was the only time in our marriage that Chris did not work full time. She devoted her time to looking after Adam and Sarah and what a good job she did. They are our children and our best friends.

I was out working a lot when our children were young, and feel that I missed quite a bit of those early years but I was able to build up and make secure our business, looking forward to and thoroughly enjoying those times when we were together.

As well as retail work, we started to get enquiries regarding event work. Our first job was the Doncaster Motor Show, held at Doncaster Racecourse. The various dealers displayed their vehicles throughout the stands and over the three days, several thousand potential buyers came to view the cars.

At the time, *Star Wars* was all the rage, and a Darth Vader character paraded through the show with a couple of Stormtroopers. I walked some distance in front of them to make sure they weren't held up and I remember that Chris turned up with the kids. It's surprising how far you go up in your children's opinion when they realize you are Darth Vader's minder!

On the second day of the show, there was a queue forming outside, prior to opening. At the front of the queue was a very tall, painfully thin man, who looked distinctly odd.

The first vehicles on view were prestige models, including a brand new Rolls Royce, priced at £49,000. The dealer asked me to keep an eye on the tall man as he had spent quite a lot of time looking at this car on the previous day and was, in his opinion, weird.

The doors opened and the crowd came in. The tall man, who was carrying a briefcase, approached the dealer and said:

'I'd like that car please.'

'It's £49,000, sir,' said the dealer.

'Will cash be okay?' came the reply.

'Oh yes, sir,' said the dealer as the man opened the case, displaying wads of high denomination cash. It turned out that this man was one of the earliest techie millionaires. These days, he would be called a geek. Never judge a book by its cover.

It was now late summer in 1983. All was going well in my new business. I had, by now, opened an office in Mexborough, renting it from a well-established Alarms and CCTV installer. I had partnered him on a few contracts, with him supplying the electronic and technical stuff, and me providing the manpower.

The phone rang. It was Pete. He was in South Yorkshire and he needed to meet me urgently.

I met him in a small hotel near Pontefract, just off the A1. He was not alone. With him was a man whose face I knew from numerous TV news programs and pictures in the newspapers. It was Ian McGregor. He had been appointed Chairman of the National Coal Board. This was after a highly controversial time at the British Steel Corporation and British Leyland; he was known to be a ruthless hatchet man.

NUM leader Arthur Scargill in negotiations with Ian McGregor, the Chairman of the National Coal Board in 1984.

After we were introduced, Pete poured us all coffee. McGregor was not a man for small talk, and he went straight to the point. He explained to me that he was expecting a major confrontation with the NUM, the mineworkers' union, before the end of the year. He expected the dispute to be long and bitter. He had no confidence in the police; likewise he had no confidence in the big security firms such as G4 or Securicor. Equally, he considered his own management staff inept.

McGregor told me that I had been identified to him by Pete as a person who could get things done, and would I look into the possibility of providing a security service to all the South Yorkshire pits during the impending dispute? The remit was to ensure that coal stocks were protected as well as colliery surfaces generally, to prevent occupation by union activists and others.

We discussed the number of men needed for the job and I confirmed that we could do it. The collieries included Cortonwood, Wath, Manvers Coal Preparation Plant, Silverwood, Yorkshire Main, Kiveton, Treeton, Kilnhurst and Barnburgh. I suggested that we deployed three men per shift to secure the pit top per colliery, supported by mobile teams who were able to respond when necessary. McGregor asked me when we could deploy and I told him, slightly holding my breath.

'Christmas.'

McGregor looked at Pete who nodded and replied that this was acceptable – but no later.

I still do not know what happened in other parts of the coalfield; certainly we had nothing to do with anything other than the South Yorkshire area, but, as Cortonwood was central to that coalfield, it is not unlikely that McGregor felt that his efforts could best be targeted there.

I was interested in the relationship between Pete and McGregor. I understand that they went back a long way, to when McGregor was trying to sort out a steel firm in the US. The Mafia had got involved in some way, and McGregor was threatened. Big Pete was either the go-between or the man who made them back off. In any case, it had worked and the relationship between the two men was trusting and strong. Clearly Pete was McGregor's fixer when things were awkward. McGregor had the contacts in the corridors of power, reporting directly to Peter Walker, the Secretary of State for Energy and, I believe, to Thatcher herself. Pete's networking skills were even darker and deeper than that.

I was given a substantial amount of money and I moved my office to one that was easily defensible in case of attack. I started to recruit and train security staff.

I formed a nucleus of men from existing contacts in the Sheffield area. Frankly, if I was doing it now, it would be difficult. These were the days before licensing and it is fair to say that I recruited a number of lads whom I would have difficulty in clearing a thorough vetting. Thugs? Maybe, but they were my thugs.

A retainer every week kept the lads sweet. Regular visits to the coalfields made them familiar with the area and I tasked them to do some quiet recruiting of their own as well.

In October 1983, we started our rollout, as the NUM called an overtime ban. Where in-house surface security staff was unavailable, we manned the collieries. This experience was invaluable, as over the next six months as the situation worsened and intensified, we got to know the nooks and crannies of the places we were to protect.

In March 1984, the strike started. Within an hour, all of the South Yorkshire area collieries were manned. There were still some manpower shortages but we were soon up to strength.

McGregor had been wrong in one regard. The police were actually very well prepared, and we actually had a very quiet first few months, as the flying pickets tried again and again to disrupt the Nottinghamshire and Derbyshire miners who refused to follow Scargill. It was only as the summer days lengthened and those activists who had been involved in aggressive picketing returned to South Yorkshire that we had any confrontations, but even then, they were short-lived.

I made it clear to the NUM officials that we would respect their picket lines as long as they respected my contract. I told them that our intention was to ensure that at the end of the strike, the colliery surfaces would be fit for purpose and the coal stocks protected.

Discretion is not something I like to see in respect to security work. We need to be pedantic and see things in black and white. However, many of the striking miners depended on coal-fired heating throughout their houses. One day, I was walking around the coal stocks of one of the collieries with a couple of security guards, when we encountered a man filling a bag with coal. I asked him what he was doing. He replied that he had worked at this particular pit for over twenty years. He needed coal to heat his water because his wife wanted a bath, and he was getting some coal, whether we liked it or not.

I turned to my colleagues and asked them what they thought. The reply was very straightforward: they were not prepared to stop the man; indeed, if he wanted a lift home with the coal, they would give him one. I concurred, on the proviso that if we found he was back tomorrow with a Transit and forty empty bags, we would arrest him. I don't think many miners went cold that winter. I do know that a large number of non-NCB employees who came to steal for profit from as far away as Blackpool were handed over to the police.

In September 1984, I met with Pete and a man called Bill Field. Bill was another freelance security man from the US who also worked for McGregor. They told me that they were about to start a back-to-work campaign which would involve delivering letters to persons who had expressed an interest in returning to work, giving them instructions where to meet and what to expect.

I was quite concerned about taking this job on. We were not there as strike breakers, and had got to know and respect the strikers and in many ways sympathized with their situation. We had got into the habit of delivering a few beers to the picket huts on Saturday nights. Sometimes fish and chips would appear, delivered by a security man. I am not trying to make out that we were popular, but we were not hated. I turned the job down. It did happen, but I believe that the NCB management did the job themselves.

At this same meeting, Bill Field showed me some pictures of men and women and asked if I had seen them. I had not.

It was explained to me that these people were suspected members of Baader-Meinhof and other terrorist groups with links to the Angry Brigade and similar UK-based factions. It was stated clearly that the authorities believed these people to have close connections with members of the NUM and that they were thought to be in the UK. Field was particularly interested, as it was thought that these terrorists had targeted British recruits, ostensibly for attacks on US installations in Europe.

Shortly after the meeting, persons purporting to be a German TV crew were detained on the Manvers Coal Preparation plant and were taken away in handcuffs. We heard no more about this, but the two incidents seemed uncomfortably related.

About this time, I met a couple of "Ruperts". These were the posh Oxford and Cambridge types that used to, and maybe still do, get jobs in the intelligence service due to daddy being in the right club or mumsie "knowing someone".

They had a tape, which had been covertly recorded, they said, at a known hotbed of NUM activity. The problem was they could not understand the accents! It must have sounded like Urdu or Swahili to them. How these two plonkers got this job I will never know but I went along with them.

I dutifully put on the earphones and listened as two men discussed the annual fishing club presentation, due to be held at a working men's club. It appeared they were not happy with the venue and were discussing alternatives. It went something like this:

'Ah dun't like ale at Waggon – it's like hosspiss.' *(The beer at the Wagon and Horses pub tastes like equine urine.)*

'Well thiv got big room though, Jud.' *(There is a room large enough to cater for the occasion, George.)*

'Can't we gu tut welfare?' *(Should we not consider the Miners' Welfare Hall at the Working mens club?)*

'Wi not welcome and it wo crap last year.' *(We are deemed to be socially unacceptable and the standards were low last year.)*

'Ars tha mean it wo crap?' *(Please explain why you thought the standards were low.)*

'Snap – potted dog an' black puddin' shite.' *(The buffet was comprised of potted meat and black pudding. I do not feel this was appropriate.)*

'Wat's tha want then?' *(Please suggest a suitable alternative.)*

'Owt but that.' *(Most places we could utilize would be an improvement on our last experience.)* 'A pint and two hayves – £1.50 – its fooking robbery.' *(The cost of drinks is exorbitant.)*

And on it went.

As the tape ended, I screwed up my face and tried not to laugh.

Turning to the Ruperts, I explained to them that it was not commonly known, but that in South Yorkshire, we had a patois totally different from Cockney rhyming slang but intended for the same purpose: to have a secret conversation that if overheard could not be understood. I went on to say that I was familiar with the Rotherham version but that this was Barnsley, a patois of such complexity and depth that only a native would understand it.

They looked like two explorers who, having discovered a foreign land, realised that all their training and previous knowledge had come to nought and they may as well be in a parallel universe. They promised to send me a copy of the tape for translation but it never arrived. I suspect that someone marked their card and they departed back to that large building near the Thames.

Orgreave, like Hillsborough, has become the opening word of many a mighty tome on police brutality, criminality and bad practice. I witnessed the "battle". There was a lead up to it that I think to some may be a little instructive in the atmosphere that prevailed in that difficult summer.

We did not provide a security service to the Orgreave Coking plant. However, we did look after the old colliery which ran down Colliery lane to the rear of the coking plant. We also had a non NCB client further up Orgreave Lane.

About a week before the "battle", I was sat drinking tea with the four pickets and the single security man who manned the picket line at the colliery, when a number of NUM activists approached. They would not engage with us at all and indeed, were somewhat annoyed at the fact that their members were prepared to speak to "outsiders" such as us.

Taking the NUM members to one side, they told them to be careful over the next week or so as they were going to 'have a showdown' with the cops and shut down the coke works. In doing so, they intended to 'give the cops a good kicking'.

We knew therefore that the NUM were going to provoke a confrontation that, whilst their intention was to close the plant, they intended to take the police on directly and defeat them.

When the day came, they tried, and failed. The police were ready because the NUM leaked like a sieve. If we knew what was going to happen, so did the police. I read once that MI5 bugged Scargill and his officials and that various places where they met were equally infiltrated. I imagine that was true. That wasn't necessary, however. Everyone knew what the NUM's plans were because those members who secretly despised what Scargill's actual ambitions were, ensured that those who needed to know got to know.

In Darnall, I once heard it said that if you went out looking for trouble, found it, and got a good hiding as a result, the best thing to do was to keep quiet about it. To those who demand an enquiry into the police's handling of the "battle", that's not a bad dictum.

As autumn approached, it appeared that the strike was going nowhere. Men were giving up and returning to work. We were kept busy, not confronting strikers but trying to ensure that the colliery surfaces were protected. Little did we know that the government intended to flatten them all anyway.

In March 1985, it was all over. I met with Pete and we shook hands and wished each other well. I never saw Pete again. He returned to the USA.

Bill Field had been a colleague of Pete's back in my time of late night trips to Runcorn. Bill was a director of a major military services contractor in Iraq and Afghanistan. I met him during a trip to Beijing, prior to the Olympics being held in that city.

He told me that Pete was alive and well, that he had married and was living in retirement in California. Despite the rise of social media, Pete has never surfaced on Facebook Twitter or anywhere else. Like all the villains or antiheroes in my tale, I liked Pete. To be honest, I was more relaxed when he wasn't around, but his presence summoned intrigue, excitement and purpose. I do miss him.

I was now looking forward to a quieter life, providing store detectives and other retail security services. It was not to be. Within an hour of the strike being called off, I received orders from the National Coal Board to take over security at all Doncaster area collieries too, effectively doubling the requirement. They had realised that, strike or no strike, there were huge security problems at their premises.

The problem was that there was no concept of loss. There was a culture within the nationalized organisation that had little or no consideration for cost. Anything that was lost, stolen or damaged was of no importance, and the tax payer would pick up the bill.

One example was when I arrived at a small colliery in Doncaster area and got into a conversation with a group of employees, including management. I was asked why we were there. I explained that during the strike, over a three-day period, £60,000 of wooden chocks had been stolen: that is a huge amount of wood. The response was:

'What's £60,000 to the NCB?' In that one reply was the reason the government had to sort the industry out: it was losing huge amounts of public money.

The South Yorkshire pit surfaces were protected pretty well, but we had failures. One night, thieves started up heavy excavating equipment and demolished the colliery offices at Thurcroft; a few days later, a striking miner was killed when a tunnel he had built to access coal from a spoil tip collapsed on him.

I remember standing there when the rescue services, the NUM and NCB officials had all gone, the body had been recovered and everyone had left the scene.

I looked around at the bleak abandoned landscape, testament to the country's declining industrial base, with no one there apart from me and perhaps the spirit of the unfortunate miner who had merely been trying to heat his home.

I thought of Scargill and Thatcher at that moment, of McGregor and Big Pete, and wondered what they were doing and whether they gave a thought to the deceased man's family. I then went home to my family, and held them close.

Chapter 6: Horses for Courses

Me and Chris with billionaire businessmen the Hinduja Brothers.

Up to now, the security business had been run as a sole proprietorship. I had a fair old pot of cash, but was not quite sure how to take the business forward.

I then had the great good fortune to meet Giles Brearley. As I look back, I regard him in the same way I regard Brendan Ingle; an eccentric genius. I sat with him and explained my situation and he immediately set up my limited company and provided the advice and guidance that helped to make our business a success. With his partner Gavin Mackinder, he set up our financial systems.

Christine, always the brains of the outfit, set up our operational systems, and, realizing that the NCB work would soon die off, I set about making appointments with new prospective customers.

I soon realised that there was a receptive customer base, which was tired of poor service and low standards. We quickly started to diversify, with a variety of customers ranging from racecourses to yoghurt manufacturers.

One customer was involved in the manufacture and distribution of carpets. It was a rapidly expanding business and the client required us to provide a gatehouse and a full access control service barrier with CCTV etc.

I appointed a gatehouse Security Officer to check all incoming/outgoing visitors and vehicles and to take an overview of the security of the site. His name was George, a former soldier, an NCO injured during the Borneo emergency. He walked with a slight limp, but was fit, focused and determined to do a good job. He irritated the somewhat unruly workforce by making them clock in and out, and the middle management by conducting regular indiscriminate car searches, but he delighted the senior management with his strict implementation of the rules they had agreed with us.

George was a single man of simple tastes: he socialized in the British Legion Club, followed his beloved Yorkshire Cricket Club and read avidly, mostly military history.

The client was a family firm. The founder was still alive but retired; his daughter had married and her husband, something of a city type, had taken over the business and was responsible for its growth. He and his wife had two children and from time to time, the kids would accompany their mother to the factory site to see their father. On these visits, the children would spend time with George in the gatehouse, whilst their mum went into the corporate offices. George grew fond of the family, as they did of him.

One day, they decided to throw a garden party at their somewhat palatial home and many of the staff were invited, including George, despite his contractor status. He arrived, and taking a beer, sat in the garden taking in the sights.

He noticed a very attractive lady being shown a lot of attention by the son-in-law and soon found out that she was a Spaniard, representing a major investor, which the company needed to fund its next expansion.

Whilst George was pleased to see that the son-in-law was working well, he could not help but notice that he was perhaps a little over-attentive. He also noticed the daughter looking somewhat concerned and slightly upset, but he thought little of it. The party ended and George returned home, and then came the commencement of the working week.

In the middle of the following week, the son-in-law, accompanied by the Spanish lady, left the factory to fly to Belgium to conduct a negotiation regarding the importation of carpets.

The meetings went on for some time and it was Saturday, when, unannounced, they returned. The factory was empty and George was, in fact, the only person on the site. The couple went into the offices, after telling George they had work to do on a major presentation.

George admired the dedication and hard work being displayed by the senior managers, and was delighted to be party to the information regarding the presentation.

He then secured the site and settled down to watch the CCTV whilst listening to the Test Match on the radio.

A few hours went by, and then the daughter and the kids turned up. She was carrying a picnic basket and said she had made sandwiches and a drink for the workers and asked if George could look after the kids for a while.

George was delighted and he shared his biscuits and made some milky tea, whilst their mother walked purposefully towards the office door.

It was only a few minutes before the first shot rang out. This was followed by the office door being flung open and a terrified son-in-law, completely naked, sprinted up the car park towards the gatehouse.

He was followed by an equally naked Spanish lady, screaming in Andalusian, who instead of following her fellow nudist, veered to her left and ran into woodland.

The daughter followed them, and, carrying the wartime Luger pistol her father had inherited, she took careful aim and shot her husband in his left buttock.

George was somewhat concerned, told the kids to lie down and stay down and went out to confront the betrayed mother of two.

He positioned himself between them and reminded the lady that her kids were in the building behind him. He reached out for the gun and as the son-in-law fainted through a mixture of terror and loss of blood, she surrendered it to him.

Following his assignment instructions, George phoned the emergency services and our Control Room, who in turn told me.

I set off, hotfoot, to the client's premises. I arrived there in about thirty minutes, just in time to see the police dog handler and his dog, escorting a hysterical Spanish lady from the wood. She was still stark naked, and the dog's inquisitiveness led to him sniffing inappropriately, leading to further distress.

Grandmother and grandfather arrived and took charge of children, and their mum was placed in handcuffs and led away.

George, in a state of shock, sat with the assignment instructions across his lap.

'I'm really sorry about this, boss,' was his first statement. He looked down at the document. 'It says in here that any visitors should be held in the gatehouse until the host is informed. I just thought it would be alright.'

I informed him that under the circumstances, the incident would not be recorded as a non-conformance under our quality system. He seemed relieved.

A Constant security colleague looking after George Michael's 30th birthday party.

I was in the office one day when I received a call from an old police colleague, who by now was a very senior police officer, asking to see me urgently.

I invited him to visit and within an hour, he arrived. With him was another man, who was introduced to me as being a CID officer with the Royal Ulster Constabulary.

It transpired that they were involved in the relocation of a man who had been of great help to the RUC in the detection and prevention of very serious crimes by Protestant paramilitaries. I will call the man Ernie.

Ernie had been born into a hard-line unionist family in Belfast. His brother was a convicted killer. Sickened by the ongoing violence, he had decided to do something about it and had approached the RUC, offering to help. They had used him in a number of operations and it was believed that he had prevented the murder of a large number of Catholics.

His last operation had involved him in taking part in a bank robbery, the funds to be used to purchase arms and explosives. Ernie had set the operation up, and to maintain his credibility, he would be arrested and tried alongside his co-conspirators.

The operation went perfectly. No one was injured, and all the team were taken into custody. Ernie was kept on remand for some months and faced trial with the others, being found guilty. It was expected that as the others were imprisoned, Ernie would be relocated.

Somehow, immediately after the trial, the defence barristers discovered that Ernie was the informer and they told his co-conspirators. His life was in serious and imminent danger and he was spirited away, ostensibly to Canada. Instead, he was sent to South Yorkshire. Accommodation for him was found and I was asked to give him a job.

To say I was wary would be an understatement, but the RUC officer assured me that Ernie was a good man and would not let me down.

I agreed. It was one of the best decisions I ever made. Ernie would only work at night. He kept himself to himself but made good mates within the company. After about ten years, he met a widowed lady with a young family of lads. He was a fantastic surrogate father to those boys, and was a truly great security man.

He had a way of instilling confidence in clients. He was always fastidious in his appearance, positive in his attitude and was both fair and firm in the way he dealt with anyone. He was an example of how all security officers should be.

I learned from him that his attitude to being a security man was that when he was assigned to a client's site, he owned it for the period he was there. His job was to protect the property, people and profits.

If the client made a product, it was his job to ensure that no criminal act would prevent that process; if they provided a service and had visitors, the impression he gave reflected on the client and the service he provided. I try my best to instil Ernie's attitudes into anyone joining the company.

When SIA licensing came into the security industry in 2005, Ernie had been with me for over fifteen years. He got his license without a problem. He renewed it in 2008, again without any problem. Then, after being criticized for the way it seemingly dished out licenses like confetti, the SIA started to refuse them to people with criminal convictions, and in 2011, although Ernie had never served a day in prison and had only engaged in criminal activity with the connivance of the RUC, Ernie was refused a renewal.

He was very upset when he told me about what had happened and I immediately tried to contact the Chairman of the SIA, Baroness Henig. I had met the Baroness a few times in my capacity as Chairman of the Police and Public Services section of the British Security Industry Association.

I was put through to her assistant and outlined the problem. Clearly this young man did not see the pending unemployment of a man who had risked his life and given up his family and friends in the national interest as a priority.

I was told that I should write explaining the situation and that the issue would be considered under the relevant appeals procedure.

I told him that Ernie would either get his license renewed by five o clock that day, or I would be speaking to every newspaper, TV station and other media outlet, explaining how this Home Office Department treated heroes.

I don't think this young fellow was used to dealing with angry Yorkshiremen representing outraged Ulstermen. I was promised a call back and received one a few minutes later: the license was approved. All very well, but I do sometimes wonder how many good men have been treated this badly and without representation, had to stand for it.

I suppose in the years I have been in this business, we have employed thousands of people, full and part time.

At the end of the pit strike, we were able to recruit large numbers of ex-miners. Their social skills tended to be a little bit too straightforward for some, their appearance could also be a little less smart than I would have liked, but when it came to the important stuff: Health and Safety, punctuality, teamwork and honesty, there were no better men.

Later, we took redundant glass blowers and steelworkers as the industrial base of the country continued to shrink.

At the same time, we started to actively recruit young men; the same lads whom, in previous generations, would have gone into the collieries, the steelworks and the glass manufacturers. Admittedly, our jobs were not as good; the pay and perks did not compare with what had been earned by their forebears in heavy industry.

Some of these young men have stayed with us and now make up our management and supervisory staff; others remain as security men. The passing of time has seen pay, conditions and prospects improve dramatically in our industry, largely down to legislation, but also because the majority of clients see the benefit of good, well-motivated security staff protecting their premises, people and profits (thanks, Ernie).

A number of my recruits have gone on to join the police and emergency services and I have taken great satisfaction in seeing their success.

One young man came to us in his early twenties; clearly an intelligent fellow, but unsure about his future. His first assignments involved him working alongside two ex-cops, actually two old pals of mine, whom I had recruited on their retirement to help us with training.

The young lad revelled in their war stories and clearly fancied joining the police. The problem was that his father and brother were both as bent as hairpins. He rightly suspected that he would be unlikely to be appointed in South Yorkshire whilst his family contained active criminals. We encouraged him to apply elsewhere and he got into the Greater Manchester force.

Years later, I was visiting a client in Manchester and was held up at a red light on a dual carriageway. Alongside me, a GMP Range Rover pulled up.

The constable in the passenger seat lowered his window and tapped on my side window. I lowered it and he asked:

'Have you been drinking, sir?'

To which I answered: 'It's ten o' clock in the morning, of course I haven't been drinking.'

'My Sergeant says you are a well-known alcoholic from South Yorkshire,' he countered.

As he said this, he leaned back and there sat the young man I had employed all those years ago, with three stripes on his arm and a broad smile on his face. I was so proud of his achievement and of those in my company who gave him direction and a vision.

Our Events section has been an important part of our business, ever since we commenced trading. I actually took small teams of response staff to York Racecourse as early as 1981. We only really started to build this side of the business after the Miners' Strike, and at the time of writing, still provide our staff on race days to the majority of the northern racecourses.

In 1994, we were asked to provide staff to Aintree, following the debacle of the Red Flag incident, when Animal Rights supporters had invaded the track, the jockeys had disobeyed the starter and set off flouting the rules. The race had been abandoned and the whole event descended into farce.

Briefing the team before a major racing event in North Yorkshire.

We were asked to provide a hundred staff. We were all ready, and then four days before the event, the client decided to double the manpower requirement! I was desperate, as we were the only contractor that actually vetted staff. This was in the days pre-licensing and to say the standards were low is a massive understatement. Some of our so-called "competitors" would literally employ anybody.

I was not prepared to deploy un-vetted staff and said so.

I received a call from Ned Kelly, who was in charge of security at Manchester United. He had been made aware of my dilemma, and told me that United did not have a game on Aintree week and he could supply the staff I needed.

These were experienced vetted football stewards and he undertook to vouch for all of them. Ned had a good reputation and I accepted his offer.

On the Thursday and Friday, the meeting went very well and I felt very relaxed working with Ned and his team.

On the Friday evening, I was approached by the catering manager responsible for the huge beer tent in the Embankment area, which only opened on the Saturday. He wanted to confirm his ten bouncers for the following day. This was the first I had heard of this. I had no one to deploy: it was known to be a rough crowd, and I had been labouring under the impression that the caterers had made their own arrangements.

Ned was ex Special Forces; a very tough cookie. He overheard the conversation, saw me pulling my hair out and stepped in:

'Don't worry, mate, leave this one to me.' He pulled out his mobile phone and was soon speaking to someone. He ended the call, and told me not to worry, as a team would be here for ten o' clock next morning.

Promptly at ten, a minibus pulled up and out stepped ten small to medium-sized chaps, who were all very fit-looking. They shook hands with Ned and he introduced them to me. I noticed their very firm handshakes. They then deployed to the embankment tent.

The day passed without incident and we were packing up to leave, when the catering manager approached me.

'Where the hell did you get those security men from?'

I asked if there had been a problem and he told me that at first, the crowd had been its usual rowdy self, but within minutes, the troublecausers had been unceremoniously bounced or spoken to in a very firm manner, and it was the quietest, best-behaved crowd he had ever known at the National. I turned to Ned and asked him where they were from. His one word answer was enough.

'Hereford.'

Many in our industry and elsewhere have served with distinction in the armed forces, the police and emergency services and some in the Special Forces.

Others claim to have done so but in truth, have never faced an angry man.

I can say with absolute honesty that I subcontracted the Beamish Embankment Beer tent to the SAS. They were very good.

A small Constant Security Team, about to be deployed at a racecourse.

The one day at Aintree I will never forget was the day we had to abandon due to an IRA threat, and send 75,000 people home without seeing the race.

It was 1997. An election had been called and there had been numerous terrorist incidents in the weeks leading up to the Grand National. On the day, all went well. Ned's team was again working with us and we had an excellent Police Liaison

Officer in Inspector Bob Smith, and a first class racecourse representative in Julien Thick, who later went on to manage with distinction at Kempton Park, then as MD at Aintree before moving to his present position as MD at Newbury.

As we got near to the start of the race, there was a slight disturbance in the Canal Turn enclosure that had to be dealt with. As was the form, I went over to Inspector Smith and Julian to tell them that all was now quiet and we were ready for the race.

I saw that Bob was involved in a serious conversation on his radio. I gave him a thumbs-up sign, indicating that all was in order. I was concerned to see his reply was a thumbs down. Something was clearly up.

His words to me were:

'We are all going home, Mick me lad, but we have to get this lot out first.'

There had been a credible bomb threat. In those days, that meant that a bomb had been planted and would operate either via a timing device or a remote signal. Seconds later, the Tannoy operated, telling people to leave the course.

The vast majority of the public were confined within the Embankment enclosure. The Police wanted all the pubic to leave via the Steeplechase area, which meant that the five gates leading from the Embankment had to be opened.

A course official had the keys, but he had disappeared. The crowd were advancing on the gates and we had no way of opening them. I was at the Canal Turn and could hear over our radio the increasing sense of urgency.

John Angel, an old friend from Sheffield city centre pub days, has a wealth of experience in dealing with large crowds and he was working with us on the day, operating a response team from a mini bus. John attended at the Embankment at speed and, using the heavy duty wire cutters we had thankfully had the foresight to bring, quickly cut down the fence, allowing access onto the racecourse.

Over 75,000 people were evacuated on foot from the stands, through ourselves to the Anchor Bridge, where they were met by Liverpool emergency services and taken to places of safety. Once they were out, we secured the perimeter and commenced a search, looking for possible explosive devices. I had about two hundred people there that day, some recruited only a few weeks before the event, but many old stagers.

The police had triggered an action which prevented the use of mobile phones, which was perfectly understandable, but the inability of some of our younger colleagues to contact loved ones at home to let them know they were okay, upset them somewhat and in one case led to a short term panic. One of the lads was a Londoner, who had only recently relocated to South Yorkshire. His wife was heavily pregnant and was at home in Mexborough. She knew no one around her to call on, and he was becoming increasingly frustrated and panicky about his wife's welfare.

By now I had all the guys (men and women) together in the centre of the Steeplechase, awaiting further orders. It looked as though we were going to have to stay there all night. The lad started to lose it. We were all a bit fraught, knowing that there may be bombs near to us. He looked at me and said:

'I know what you are going to do. You are going to leave us to it – you are going to get into your car and drive away leaving, us all here.'

There was no sense to this statement but the lad was clearly very scared. I sensed two hundred pairs of eyes on me and realised that my response was either going to calm everyone or panic them more.

I put my hand on his shoulder; he was now in tears. I made him look at me and I told him that when we left, we would all leave together, that I would be at the back of the column of minibuses, not at the front, and that he was to stop worrying.

One or two of the older, wiser heads stepped in to reassure him further and he started to calm down.

Time went by, and at about 9.45pm, Bob Smith and some other cops came to us, stating that the racecourse was to be put under complete lockdown at 10pm, and that if we could get out by then, they would appreciate it as they now wanted to run the race on the following Monday and would need our guys back early on Monday morning.

Two hundred security guards got onto the fifteen or so minibuses and headed out over Anchor Bridge. I hung back, just in case of any stragglers taking one last run around the perimeter. As I got to Anchor Bridge, now deathly quiet, I was stopped by a solitary police officer. He ascertained who I was and asked me to go as quickly as possible to the M67 slip road as there was a problem with our staff.

It was now a nineteen-hour day and I was facing a two-hour trip back to South Yorkshire. The last thing I wanted was more hassle. I got to the slip road to find all the minibuses parked on the hard shoulder.

I pulled up in front of them and exited the vehicle to find out what was going on. The supervisors were grouped together with wry smiles on their faces as I approached. I asked what was going on and was told that the staff had said that as I was not prepared to leave without them, they were not prepared to leave without me. It was a truly humbling, emotional moment.

We drove back to Mexborough in convoy. All the guys were asked if they would be prepared to work the following Monday. Some could not due to full-time work commitments, but everybody who could make it volunteered.

Constant security staff conducting anti-terror searches at Aintree in 2016.

Every one of them turned up and the Grand National 1997 was run on the Monday afternoon.

One of the main reasons our guys were so positive was not my inspirational leadership, impressive as this surely was. It was the fact that while all the mobile phones were inoperable, Chris had managed, via South Yorkshire police, to find out we were all safe. She then went into our Mexborough control room and with the assistance of other office-based colleagues rung all wives, girlfriends and family members to let them know their loved ones were safe.

Incidentally, our cockney couple had a daughter. Lovely kid, speaks Yorkshire. I have no idea which horse won – I don't care. The IRA caused minor inconvenience, and it gave me a memorable experience, one I will never forget.

From time to time, we have had staffing issues and it has been necessary to cast our employment net quite widely. In 2005 Chris, together with our children Sarah and Adam, accompanied by our HR Director Michael Booth went to Poland to recruit staff. They took on about twenty-five men from diverse backgrounds, including a lawyer, a journalist, a retired Colonel, a Merchant Marine Communications Officer, and other top quality personnel.

They joined the company, and most of them are still here, some marrying or bringing over wives and girlfriends. Our first baby was a little girl and we sent her mother a bouquet of white carnations and white roses. The national flower of Poland mingled with the White Rose of Yorkshire. Getting to know them was an education. The Colonel had served in Iraq, alongside British and US fighting units, and the seaman had been in the middle of the "Perfect Storm", the phenomenal weather event that prompted the film starring George Clooney and Brad Pitt. Twenty-five men, with twenty-five stories.

Later, we employed a number of ex Gurkha soldiers, again a great bunch of guys, who whilst they fear nothing, have to be guided somewhat to the more refined aspects of British culture.

For instance, we were doing a short-term job for the Environment Agency to protect some expensive equipment situated at a fishing spot on the Trent. I received a call from the client asking me to ensure that our Gurkha colleague brought sandwiches for lunch rather than trapping, killing and skinning rabbits and then roasting them over an open fire. Apparently the fishermen were delighted and happy to join him, adding their own catch to the feast!

A celebration with the Gurkha community in Doncaster.

One day I was in our Control Room and our Polish call handler was trying to tell a Nepalese colleague how to negotiate the Leeds one way system, in English. As I listened, I was reminded of the old comedians Al Read and Bob Newhart, whose stock in trade was to deliver to the audience one side of a telephone conversation. It was hysterically funny. Having said that, the one way system was navigated successfully.

It has been an absolute joy to work with all those who have come to us and represented the company, the town and the county so positively, to see them grow in confidence, sometimes leaving when the job they really want comes along, often staying with us and developing into supervisors and managers. Or maybe they are content and satisfied to be that person who increasingly becomes an integral part of the thin blue line that protects and defends our infrastructure, our factories, offices and sporting venues: the Security Man.

This is one Security Man's tale.

Printed in Great Britain
by Amazon